DOU

CW00920014

CENT~~UKI~~

THE STORY OF TWO UNIQUE
MANX TRAMWAYS

by

Stan Basnett* and
Keith Pearson

*Mr Basnett is responsible for Chapter 4

Dedicated to the memory
of Reginald Orton
187(9) – 1955

A catalogue for this book is available from the British Library

ISBN 1 874422 17 6 Softback
      1 874422 18 4 Hardback

Published 1996 by
Adam Gordon
Priory Cottage
Chetwode
Nr Buckingham
MK18 4LB

Printed by The Amadeus Press Ltd,
517 Leeds Road, Huddersfield HD2 1YJ

Typesetting by Highlight Type Bureau Ltd,
2 Clifton Villas, Bradford BD8 7BY

Contents

List of Illustrations

Colour Section

Personal Introduction

The two centenaries which are marked by this book effectively commemorate vanished undertakings which, at their inception, technically represented the opposite poles of obsolescence and innovation. For the writer, it is perhaps disconcerting to realise that a first tenuous personal 'sighting' of one of the lines concerned took place just over half a century ago.... The commencing dates of public service on the two tramways concerned were 7th August (Douglas Southern Electric Tramway)* and 15th August (Upper Douglas Cable Tramway) but the ensuing text details other 'occasions' which (respectively) ante and post dated these two dates.

For the writer, the especial 'magic' of the Island's tramways was perhaps epitomised by the DHMD's 'ghost' tramway, first personally encountered in 1949 (more distant glimpses in 1945 were of the line's still intact overhead – a tantalising view from an IMR train!). The pedestrian access then available allowed a full length (appx. 3 miles) traverse of the entire Marine Drive. It is still a lovely piece of coastline, and the original relatively modest scale of the Drive (as constructed between 1891-7) made it a somehow unobtrusive element in the total scene. The rock faces were by this time fully weathered so that the 'rawness' of immediate post-construction years was no longer apparent. The generally south-east facing aspect makes for rapid 'warm up' on sunny days so that the whole landscape enjoyed a private climate where plants flowered early and flourished, sheltered from the prevailing winds. The roadway was of genuine Macadam construction – e.g., carefully graded and compacted stones with no bituminous element so that its colour and texture accorded well with the surroundings. When reconstructed in 1956-63 this essential unobtrusiveness was lost. Ensuing 'fatal' technical problems (outlined in later text) were, one suspects, largely self-created by the over-application of modern technology and the corresponding absence of late-Victorian expertise (the latter derived from an intimate 'hands-on' involvement with such works by their supervisors and, perhaps, the use of gentler explosives like gunpowder). The overall ambience was that of a vast 'silence', to which the sound of seabirds and sea were mere enhancements. The former Manager, Reginald Orton, often spoke of the inherent pleasures of his job – where today would an engineer have three miles of track, major steel bridges, a power station and 16 trams and all the minor civil engineering of the Drive in his care – with seabirds, seals and (highly edible) crabs as company?

The book begins with an account of the extraordinary sequence of events, both promotional and physical, that led to the construction of the standard gauge tramway along the Marine Drive and describes its 40 seasons of operation, then continues to an account of the Upper Douglas line. The latter enjoys the distinction of being the last British cable tramway operation, and, as above, in its very technology had an initial built-in obsolescence. Its construction was typical of the fully evolved British systems of which Edinburgh was the most noted example, but from the mid-nineties there was really no technical justification for the

---

*Constructed along, and latterly owned by, the Douglas Head Marine Drive Company

installation of a cable tramway. Dick Kerr must have been quite effective propagandists to sell their system as late as 1895-6.

Returning to the Marine Drive, 1949's personal explorations had led, by summer of 1951, to a more direct 'entanglement' (even to the extent of borrowing the former Manager's boiler suit!). The writer came to spend much of the week ending 23 June 1951 in the organisation and execution of the 'rescue' of electric car No. 1 of 1896. At the time tramway preservation was barely-recognised as significant, and it says much for the far-sightedness of Island engineering professionals that their help was so unstintingly and promptly given – the initial decision to attempt a move was to be followed by its execution 5 days later.

As custodian of the car during its 5 year island storage, the writer progressively acquired a close acquaintance with the archaic technology of the period – typically, lightning arresters of early 'nineties date where the conducting path was formed by a charred groove formed across a hardwood block! This same episode was to become an 'open sesame' to the offices of Island civil engineering and tramway professionals, plus the extraordinary engineering establishment of John and James Knox – who had unhesitatingly loaned 'tram rescuing' implements to the Author, who then bicycled off to Little Ness. A special mention of the then Divisional Surveyor of the Highway Board, the late W.E. (Billy) Vick and of his colourful master Surveyor General R.C.W. Brown is a 'must' here.

Seventeen years later a more 'archaeological' operation saw the remnants of Upper Douglas cable cars 72 and 73 extracted from their Crawyn (Ballaugh) location, again with support from Island professionals and again with the help of volunteers whose friendship and sustained support has continued to 'today'.... it was to take 8 years to complete the major part of the necessary reconstruction. Thus it happens that both the 1896 lines enjoy more than mere literary representation.......

Brampton, Appleby in Westmorland, 1996
F.K. Pearson

Chapter One

The Genesis of the Marine Drive

This account is necessarily a précis of a more detailed account of the Marine Drive and the Suspension Bridge and Tower schemes by the present Author in the Journal of the Manx Museum, Vol. VII, issues 85 and 86.* The necessary permission of Manx National Heritage is here gratefully acknowledged.

The Marine Drive story in fact begins with the 'Suspension Bridge Company', more fully known as The Douglas Head Suspension Bridge and Tower (this project was perhaps the ultimate Manx expression of over-confidence in Company promotion and of the gullibility of investors at large!). It is constructive at this point to emphasise the major role as a place of resort attained by Douglas Head by the 'eighties of the last century. The area was officially a 'Recreation Ground', itself leased by the Town Commissioners from the Nunnery Estate, with which it shared a boundary wall on the southern side. The latter property belonged to Major (later Sir) John Goldie Taubman, J.P., S.H.K. The DSET were to acquire him as a Director, and the DHMD 'enjoyed' a not entirely harmonious relationship with him as their most vocal neighbour. Relations with his successor, Leigh Goldie Taubman, were even more prickly. Taubman animals who penetrated DHMD's fencing and then fell over the cliffs were inevitably of enormous value – according to LGT!

On the Head, Victorian predecessors of later more elaborate amenities saw the provision of refreshments, concert party type entertainment, 'Punch and Judy' and all the (relatively) innocent pastimes of the last quarter of the century. At its north western extremity, sea water 'baths' at Port Skillion had enjoyed instant popularity from their inception in 1874.

Access was a problem, for a long walk to the old stone bridge at the inner end of the harbour was followed by an equally lengthy ascent via the 'Head Road' more correctly 'Fort Anne Road'. En route, the properties included some dating from the Regency period, some quite grandiose. This of course assumes that the persons concerned did not make use of the ferries which plied to and fro across the harbour and which led to a steep but direct access to the Head. These ultimately included quite substantial steam ferry boats, some with a piano and other musical instruments aboard. In 1895-6 the predecessor of today's (pedestrian) swing bridge was built, operating under Government auspices, but the Marine Drive story had begun earlier, in 1889.

The chronology which follows concerns itself with the several successive 'access' schemes, an ensuing section of text dealing with the Marine Drive itself (which came to be constructed as a satellite of the Suspension Bridge and Tower concern). The significance of underlined items has already been explained, whilst a 'dagger' indicates a cross reference to the succeeding Marine Drive account.

---

*Certain minor errors exist in the originating texts as printed and these are hereafter corrected as they appear (the existence of such a correction is here indicated by underlining the wording or numerical data concerned).

The Bridge schemes: a Calendar

1885/6: Daniel Cregeen, C E (1821-1894) produces his pedestrian tunnel scheme for a crossing of the harbour.

1886: Government discusses a bridge proposal: all such schemes were constrained by the need for shipping to continue unimpeded.

1889: Manx entrepreneurs Walter Darker Pitt and G.J. Cuddon enter into partnership with Dr Wm. Abbotts and Julius W.M. Byrne and create the 'Standard Contract and Debenture Corporation', registered in July. Essentially, they purchased sites and re-sold them at a profit to SC&DC satellite companies, for whom the SC&DC also acted as (expensive) contractors (these unhappy facts took about five years to fully emerge!). Cuddon was a solicitor, Pitt what can only be described as an 'ideas' man. Expensive London offices and (rather insubstantial) Douglas ones were opened. They concurrently created/announced the schemes for an 'Eiffel' tower and a Marine Drive. †

A scheme for a harbour bridge, approached by a triangular approach ramp, 30 feet wide and with spans of 380, 410 and 300 feet – giving Head access at about 100 feet above harbour level – was already under discussion by Cregeen (and his engineers Jerram and Livingston) with the Harbour Commissioners engineer. This earlier scheme originated with W.D. Pitt.

July 1889: The SC&DC now promoted the 'Douglas Head Suspension Bridge Ltd' and 'Douglas Head Marine Drive, Ltd' with design work by one Thomas Floyd, C E (although Cregeen was still technically involved). All bridge schemes centred on sites near the present swing bridge.

W. D. Pitt stands alongside G. B. Jerram, sometime about 1891. Mr Pitt also appears in another photograph flanked by two very 'shady looking' gentlemen – alas, they could not be identified by the late Miss G. H. Pitt, who provided both these photographs and some interesting papers relating to the genesis of Blackpool Tower. A flysheet circulated by Pitt c.1900 includes (below the Tower's photograph) the wording reproduced below. The post 1891 success of the Tower under local promoters has in fact tended to obscure the less solid 'foundations' of the concern as a Standard Contract and Debenture Corporation satellite! (Abbotts was a friend of Blackpool's Dr Cocker, a locally revered 'founding father' of the resort).

'. . . The Tower, Blackpool
Founded by W. D. Pitt
The formation of the Blackpool Tower Company, Limited, and erection of the 'Eiffel Tower' and magnificent pile of buildings, as shown by the picture, was a scheme arranged by Mr W. D. Pitt. There formerly . . .'

By November major publicity for the SC&DC schemes saw Floyd meet the Governor.

14 January 1890: Floyd's plans before Tynwald. The bridge now sprang from a circular tower, combining a spiral roadway with a series of central 'halls', and surmounted by a viewing tower. A summit height of 405 feet was projected – the interior of the spiral had a radius of 46 feet. The bridge had four spans of 148, 400, 200 and 115 feet, clearing high water by 135 feet (all spans are listed N to S, as also previously quoted example). The metalwork for bridge and tower would weigh around 3,200 tons. There had been extensive discussion with the Town and the Harbour Commissioners, and with the IoM Steam Packet Co, but Tynwald rejected the scheme 13:8.

February 1890: Work on the site had seen it cleared by 7 January. Still undaunted, the promoters now came up with a rectangular tower with hydraulic lifts, totalling 375 feet in overall height. The structure was to contain about 3,700 tons of metalwork – the bridge is not mentioned – and there had been 'treaties' with the Town Commissioners and the Steam Packet Co. (This information from reportage during February).

19 April 1890: DHSB Ltd prospectus appears. The capital remained at £100,000 – of 105 founder shareholders most were from the industrial north, and only five were Manx – albeit of some distinction, in three instances. A London address accompanies the re-appearance (in particular) of Dr William Abbots, with Jerram and Livingston as Surveyors.* Meanwhile the intended incorporation of the Marine Drive Company was announced, scheduled for 9th July.†

May 1890: No significant work on the site – some local 'wags' begin to scent a subject for the exercise of humour.

16 October 1890: Agreement with Town Commissioners and Steam Packet Co. 'finalised'.

23/24 October 1890: Earl of Lathom, Lord Chamberlain of England and Deputy Grand Master of English Freemasonry arrives on chartered SS 'Snaefell' and following day leads ceremonial procession before laying foundation stone on site** prepared by contractor J.D. Nowell (J.D.&H.M. Nowell seem to have been major contractors working from a base in Heckmondwike – their history deserves investigation).*** Some catcalls marred the occasion – the DHSB Co was by now the subject of much suspicion on the part of the non-shareholders in Douglas! (Much criticism of 'prostitution' of Freemason's craft, etc.)

December 1890: Marine Drive 'set out' and reasonably continuous work sustained thereafter.† (On December Pitt launched his Blackpool Tower scheme using a site then owned by the SC&DC – by May 1891 the Blackpool Co was reconstructed to exclude any SC&DC 'contamination' and prospered thereafter as a genuinely local enterprise. Jerram and Livingston were still 'involved', via G.B. Jerram).

* Recent Manx Museum acquisitions (MD1302) include some Marine Drive sections by Jerram and Livingston and some building plans by Maxwell & Tuke.
** Now occupied by the IoMSPCo. goods department
*** Work on a substantial scale for the Lancashire and Yorkshire Railway works at Horwich is one known example, and the Liverpool Overhead Railway Dingle tunnel.

January to August 1891: Only 'pumping' taking place at the Tower site. Pier head amenity building erected on site once earmarked by Cregeen and Jerram for bridge approach ramp.

Mid December 1891 to early 1892: Marine Drive† Suspension Bridge and Standard Debenture concerns all in court for non-payment of debts! Cuddon petitions for liquidation of the SC&DC – of which he was originally Solicitor. There was a hearing on 7 January 1892. The liquidator was to be former Auditor Byrne – a somewhat dubious choice, some thought! Meanwhile Pitt and some others had set up a 'London Contract and Debenture Corporation' which was a replica SC&DC scheme for profitable satellite creation – an 'Eiffel Tower' and Winter Gardens for Scarborough, for example. In competition Cuddon created a 'Royal Trusts and Assets....' (etc, etc) Corporation – all parties were by now at each other's throats! DHSB tried to meet on 29 March 1892, but failed to do so and were only thereafter seen in Court. By 16 March 1893 they were, effectively, a spent force – the shareholders were to receive 12¹/₂% in 1899!

April 1892: The Douglas Head Marine Drive Company elected a new Directorate and kept their scheme going† (DHSB and SC&DC were only finally dissolved in 1923).

1893: Maxwell and Tuke (of 41 Corporation Street, Manchester) became 'architects' to the Marine Drive – and the new Blackpool Tower.†

Having outlined what the Clerk of the Rolls contemporaneously described as leaving the Island's Chancery Court 'in the dark amidst a mass of rascality and chicanery', it is now time to more fully consider the only physical accomplishment of the 'SD&DC', the Marine Drive. As seen above, a new start in April of 1892 saw men of a different calibre 'at the helm'. A son of one of these 'founding fathers', the late S.H. Davenport, sadly incinerated much of the Drive's history a few days before we made personal contact, but more happily the late O.S. Wrangham, Agent to the Nunnery Estate, located and was able to allow access to a cache of DHMD material and (even more exotically) papers left by William Sebastian Graff Baker (of whom more is to follow).

The Marine Drive

The Marine Drive Company obviously was a typical creation of the SC&DC, intended purely as a profitable satellite – as earlier implied, SC&DC contracted for the Drive's construction at a suitably enhanced rate before sub-letting contracts for the actual work to other parties, (fortunately, in the case of the Marine Drive these were of reasonable, indeed, total competence). The Memorandum and Articles of 1 July 1889 allowed, chiefly, for the construction of 'roads and or tramways' – the prospectus only emerged a year later, on 7 July 1890. The capital was to be £40,000 with 2000 founders shares, the latter with a supposed inbuilt 'bonus' capability. Like those of the DHSB, these shares were mostly taken up by investors in the Lancashire area and the later salvation of the Company from the clutches of the SD&DC was to spring from this source (readers of '100 Years of the MER' may sense a resurgence of Mancunian pride). The self-laudatory publicity of 9 July 1890 which accompanied Incorporation included a rather 'stretched' distance of 'five to six miles'. The general scheme provided for a forty foot roadway with an embattled wall on the seaward side but as construction proceeded and funds dwindled this ambitious standard was diminished, as will be evidenced from our illustrations. There was a successful mainland precedent – the Marine Drive around the Great Orme at Llandudno, which once constructed enjoyed minimal operating costs and consistent patronage.

The proposed capital of £40,000 was to be augmented by £20,000 of 4% debentures (nowhere was the fact of the Marine Drive's concession having been obtained by SC&DC and being now resold to DHMD mentioned!). A description by Jerram and Livingston(e)* was of reasonable technical accuracy but played havoc with Manx spellings.

The succeeding years are again suitable for a 'chronology', as now follows:

November-December 1890: As in DHSB notes, Drive 'set out' and construction put in hand. Commencement about a hundred yards from Woodcock's photographic studio (this building still exists).

The work was placed in the hands of H.M. Nowell and appears to have begun about 13 December (up to the Nunnery wall the road was only 24 feet wide but 40 thereafter – at this point were intended the ornamental entrance gates and a lodgekeepers house – ultimately built to the seaward side). Immediately before the gates was one of a number of 'half (width)

'Rockmen': the central seated figures are of 'the man in charge', one Bartlett, and his young son. Several of the gang are to be seen holding 'tools of the trade'. The man at the far left seems to have deserved his nickname of 'Darkie' Hornby, whilst only the Emerald Isle could have produced a figure like that of Barney McAvoy, second from right. There is a larger group surviving, on which appear a joiner, Corlett (presumably i/c the bridge construction) and a philosophical looking individual, Ropeman Swindlehurst. With cliffs like those of Wallberry the last named must have been fully exercised. *The late Mrs M. Marshall*

*A probable mis-reporting.

Wallberry, as completed in summer of 1893. Its pitch pine timbers had a very short working life, for by 1896 it functioned as an erectors' scaffold for its steel successor. The style of Horse Leap must be assumed similar, and both structures assumedly shared broadly the same dimensions as their steel successors. The elaboration of the earlier Pigeon Stream bridge (seen later) was not repeated here!

The late Mrs M. Marshall

bridges' – a four foot footpath was provided. A 100 foot timber bridge was to be provided at Pigeon's Stream – the Drive was set out mainly along the cliff tops, until reaching the precipitous Wallberry cliffs. At the southern end the Drive was to descend behind the existing Port Soderick hotel so as to reach the existing Glen Road.

January 1891: Work force rises to 100 – Wallberry as a 'realistic' target for Easter. By May workforce up to 300 – Jerram and Livingston drove to Wallberry.

Thursday 23 July 1891: Ceremonial opening with a 50 carriage procession. Guard of Honour awaited Governor (the arrangements were handled by Jerram and Chas Maley, Co Secretary, in concert with Manager E.H. Robotham) along with Abbots and other 'notables', the Lord Bishop, and W.D. Pitt! Governor Sir Spencer Walpole was given a golden key and duly unlocked the gates – speeches in a marquee at Wallberry were of the usual order, then refreshments in another marquee (nearer Douglas) followed. Subsequently, the Drive entry charge was (as planned) 2d.

By this time J.D. Nowell was also at work.

December 1891: Jerram at work as Agent for SC&DC, DHSB and DHMD in an effort to avoid their dissolution. DHMD 'in court' (sued) by the 14th.

Thursday 28th January 1892: Crucial and uproarious meeting in Manchester where Abbots' attempts to stifle criticism are overturned by shareholder S.H. Emmott and aides Messrs. Westwell and Sykes, who imposed a Committee of Investigation to challenge the 'version of affairs' presented by Abbott's aides 'Schultz & Co., Chartered Accountants'.

April 1892: Emmott and aides create new directorate, then meet creditors and secure moratorium on existing debts (12 months, 5%). Shareholder Dr. Farrell (local raconteur – see '100 Years of the Manx Electric Railway') by now a Marine Drive propagandist and seeking an electric line from Port Soderick to Laxey!

June 1893: Drive now upheld as 'major local attraction' (wide press coverage), the scheme now including electric tramway plans very like those attained in 1896. Re-opening had been on/about 20 May with lengthy accompanying verbiage from Dr. Farrell.

'Mid' 1893: Option to construct electric tramway taken up by concessionaire – see ensuing chapter for details of these matters up to 1896.

Monday 7 August 1893: Grand re-opening at noon! – the day's admission charge 1d. H.M. Nowell had been at work on the timber bridges at Wallberry and Horseleap (spans 256 and 120 feet, 267 feet above sea level – the first had a central support) so now the 'terminus' was at Little Ness. 2,200 passed through the turnstiles.

November 1893: Some recurrent 'cashflow' problems as Keristal extension proving expensive (bad terrain). Maxwell and Tuke (earlier appointed as architects) had both died. In July 1893 Maxwell had brought in site engineer Clarke (a Swindon man) who spent the rest of his life working for the DHMD (died winter 1910-1911). He, effectively, acted as the controlling civil engineer from his arrival.

December 1894: Some progress with tramway schemes – new Drive extensions beyond the Whing are much narrower than the previous standard.

1 January 1895: DHMD office moved to corrugated iron building at Castletown Road gates. The section of the Drive from Keristal to the Castletown Road gates is totally different from any other, crossing marshy ground by a causeway. A smithy was built at Keristal, and other workshops at the Castletown Road gates. Through traffic thus made feasible by this date (unidirectional, S along Drive – see also page 18 text).

2 April 1895: In light of 'apparent' success, second debenture issue of £20,000

1897: Drive extended to Port Soderick in concert with new tramway, now again to a more generous width. (The southern end of the Drive was in fact a cul de sac for vehicles, initially, only a footpath continuing to the beach).

February 1899: T.J. Hutchinson, F.I.C., an industrial Chemist, then resident in Bury, Lancs., becomes Receiver and Manager of DHMD, whose receipts had 'nose-dived' once the Electric Tramway (built in 1896-1897) opened for business. He was to persevere at his task until a reconstruction of the inherently overcapitalised Company in 1909.

6 August 1909: Reconstructed Marine Drive Co: capital still £40,000 (issued £37,687) (Year to end 31 March 1910). Hutchinson had already reduced the debenture debt by about 40% – the new Company had no such burden (debentures).

3 April 1926: DHMD acquire Douglas Southern Electric Tramway from New General Traction Co. Earlier had put out £4,500 of debentures – some

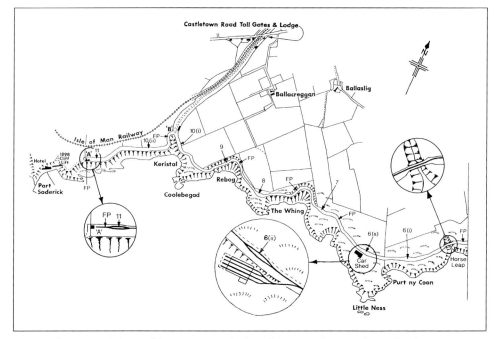

The Marine Drive and its tramway – the list of passing places explains the changes of 1908, at which date the depot layout depicted was constructed, replacing the original traverser.   *The Engineer, S. Broomfield and J. C. Cooke*

The Douglas Southern Electric Tramway:
Table of Passing Places, as numbered on plan
(the letters FP denote an electrical feeder point).

1   The Head
2   The Gates
3   Pigeon's Stream (from 'the stream of the pigeon') (in Manx)
4   The Farm
5   Wallberry
6 (i)   Little Ness (until 1908)
6 (ii)   Little Ness as relocated
7   Whing (until 1908)
8   Rebog
9   Coolebegad (until 1908)
10 (i) Keristal (until 1908)
10 (ii) Keristal as relocated
11   Port Soderick
Letters A B indicate the 1897 extension of the tramway.
Passing Places 5, 6(i), 7 and 9 all lay north of their nominal geographical locations.
The identifying arrows lead to the midpoint of each of the loops.

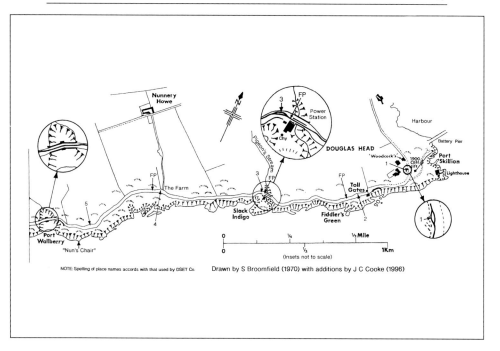

NOTE: Spelling of place names accords with that used by DSET Co.   Drawn by S Broomfield (1970) with additions by J C Cooke (1996)

'spent' on joint DSET/DHMD bridgework in 1920-21 for which payment was overdue. In general reasonable DHMD performance over the period. The Directors now included James Downs Hutchinson (son of T.J.).

To close this chapter, it has to be said that the financial performance of the DHMD forms a complex topic, in part due to non-continuous surviving records and differing modes of presentation. An extensive treatment appears on pages 154/155 of Manx Museum Journal 86, previously referred to. For the present purpose, the discrepancy between the earning power of the tramway and the Drive is well illustrated by some sample figures. In 1900, 1d per passenger from the DSET gave the Drive Co £764, whilst its own turnstiles netted a mere £156. In the boom year of 1920 the tramway paid over a total of £1805 (now comprising both the 1d/passenger and the 5% of gross receipts also payable) whilst the turnstiles netted £618 (the 1919 figures were respectively £1062 and £444).

Schedule of gradients from The Gates to Keristal, taken from 'The Engineer' of 16 October 1896. The additional table (opposite) is for the section between The Gates and the Douglas Head terminus, using the profile in 'Railway World' for January 1897. Regrettably, the last is 'crowded' to the point of illegibility.

Distance in feet.	Direction.	Gradient 1 in	Distance in feet.	Direction.	Gradient 1 in
*208	Falling	37·46	106	Falling	48·62
265	,,	45·61	§167·5	,,	59·61
110·5	Rising	110·5	133	,,	38·44
263	,,	36·32	157	,,	29·46
178·5	,,	25·25	74	,,	528·6
56	,,	88·89	112	,,	1120·0
184	Falling	37·78	80·5	,,	268·3
141	,,	36·92	44·5	,,	158·9
226	,,	30·09	55	,,	785·7
88	,,	28·94	49	,,	39·84
101	,,	246·34	214	,,	24·07
134	Rising	35·93	62	,,	72·94
38	,,	34·55	59	Rising	21·85
23	Falling	46·0	116·5	,,	42·68
†135	Rising	613·64	67·5	,,	31·10
112	,,	143·59	78·5	,,	67·67
146	Falling	34·19	125	,,	91·24
126	,,	30·58	179	,,	27·69
183	Rising	182·81	195	,,	29·02
252	,,	32·39	124	,,	23·05
153·5	,,	34·4	181	,,	28·24
150	,,	29·1	205·5	,,	26·05
30	,,	11·32	134·5	,,	33·21
228	,,	31·53	182	,,	30·90
179	,,	30·4	75	,,	25·0
112	,,	74·66	115	,,	18·87
80	,,	38·1	142	,,	11·36
209·5	,,	29·55	55	,,	32·74
120	,,	25·26	55·5	,,	74·0
221	,,	34·86	83	Falling	24·41
67	,,	33·16	130	,,	10·43
250	,,	52·2	152	,,	12·66
130	,,	28·93	100	,,	18·55
147	,,	38·68	165	,,	44·60
240	,,	26·17	265	,,	23·13
125	,,	24·08	48	,,	16·22
128	,,	18·68	151	,,	22·01
103	,,	13·59	204·5	,,	23·75
117·5	,,	20·5	65	,,	54·61
137	,,	23·34	95	,,	13·19
169	,,	26·20	44	Rising	46·81
101·5	,,	23·28	85	,,	17·0
162	,,	21·43	33	Falling	31·43
68	..	6800·0	140	,,	33·02
122·5	Falling	35·0	51	,,	33·77
‡114	,,	16·01	94	,,	23·38
123	,,	17·96	93·5	,,	20·55
48	,,	42·10	155	,,	23·42
120	,,	21·50	50	,,	33·68
111	,,	29·00	87	,,	16·44
105	,,	25·74	73·5	,,	18·66
170	,,	40·58	36	,,	31·03
			||28	..	23·14

Distance in feet (approx.)	Direction	Gradient 1 in
105	Rising	Illegible
155	Falling	191.25
135	Falling	17.2
125	Falling	27.8
125	Falling	20.5
85	Falling	53
105	Falling	47.2
125	Falling	52
85	Falling	20.5
125	Falling	50
50	Falling	24.3
208	Falling	37.46

Last item on list from 'Engineer'. (Passing loop at 'The Gates').

Key to Figure 6.

* Entrance
† Pigeon's Stream Bridge
‡ Wallberry Bridge
§ Horse Leap Bridge
ll (Keristal)

To give visual emphasis to the foregoing, here is the 'Railway World' profile, less its numbering and with an estimated portion covering Keristal – Port Soderick.

J. C. Cooke

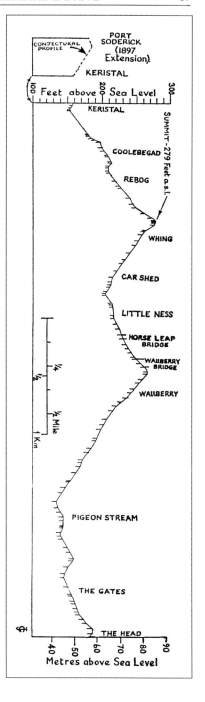

Chapter Two

The Douglas Southern

'The situation of this tramway is in some respects unique...
(DHMD advertisement, 1935)

As already outlined, the contorted Manx slates of the rugged coastline running SSW from Douglas Head presented an impressive sight, and by 1893 had been made easily accessible, whether on foot or in carriages. Once the Marine Drive opened to the gates erected on the old Castletown Road, a circular route became a popular choice for the latter conveyances, as this allowed a fairly rapid return to Douglas. A first mention of the tramway scheme on 7 August 1893 has already been mentioned, and by November of the same year the extension to Keristal and the Castletown Road, then anticipated as soon to be accomplished. However, the lateness of the 1893 re-opening (7 August was effectively mid season) found the Drive Co. short of money and architects Maxwell and Tuke* both died 'late in the year'. The completion of the extension through to the Castletown Road has not been dated, but seems to have been substantially later in 1894 than had been hoped for in the summer of '93.

Among the advocates of the tramway were two major DHMD shareholders, George William Lowcock and George Hill, partners in Lowcock, Hill & Co, electrical engineers, of Old Trafford. The unidentified concessionaire of 1893 having evidently withdrawn, Lowcock & Hill secured a new tramway concession in their own names from the DHMD company on 6 November 1894, and sought a contractor who would build their line and accept payment largely in shares. The successful candidate was the Electric & General Contract Corporation of 35 Parliament Street, Westminster, registered on 25 November 1892 to take over the electrical contracting business of William Sebastian Graff Baker, M INST E E. Graff Baker, an American citizen, was then agent for the Thomson-Houston International Electrical Company of Boston, Massachusetts and, in addition to operating the pioneer Roundhay Park electric tramway at Leeds, had secured a concession to electrify the tramways at Coventry. On 10 December 1894, Lowcock and Hill made a private agreement with Graff Baker's E&GCC granting the latter the benefit of the concession which they held from the DHMD, and which was defined on 2 April 1895 as being for ten years, after which the Marine Drive company could purchase the line or extend the lease for twenty-one years. No legislative powers were needed to build the line, as all the land was privately owned.

Meanwhile, the Marine Drive company had come to deal with the E&GCC direct. They were if anything more urgently concerned with improving access to the Drive as it then stood, and on 27 March 1895 obtained permission from (by now) Sir John Goldie-Taubman to build a 35-foot roadway down from Douglas Head (from point B to point A on the accompaning plan), and build a tramway on it, the road to remain Sir

*The firm, of 41 Corporation Street, Manchester must have continued in business as a drawing for a Castletown Road Lodge and gates under 'their' name is dated October 1894.

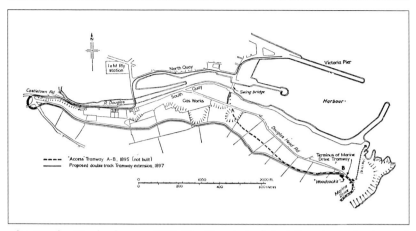

The Douglas Head schemes, 1895-97. The chain dotted line shows the 'access' tramway (extending from A to B) as proposed in 1895, the firm line the ambitious extension line to the Victoria Pier (of double track!) proposed in 1897.   *J. C. Cooke*

John's property. Almost as an afterthought, the agreement allowed DHMD to build tramways on the Drive itself, south of the Toll Gates, if they wished. DHMD had given the task of building the proposed access tramway to Graff Baker as early as 25 March 1895, and the latter thereafter dealt direct with Sir John. By February 1896 the agreement was enlarged to permit a link tramway from point B to the Toll gates (this was ultimately built as an integral part of the Marine Drive tramway) and another extension from point A down to the south side of the new harbour swing bridge. This was to be a 'mechanical tramway, railway or lift' and the gradients imply a cliff-lift type of installation.

It is convenient to deal here with the fate of the access tramway and road after mid-1896. In the winter of 1896-7, the New General Traction Company (to be described later) proposed a totally different tramway extension of a most ambitious character. The Marine Drive adhesion tramway would have been extended down to the harbour, crossing the old stone bridge and continuing to the Victoria pier (see plan); this line was not built, and with its 1 in 12 gradients and reverse curves would have been a hard line to work. The tramway terminus, in fact, remained on Douglas Head, 184ft above sea level, and an orthodox cliff lift was ultimately built by a private investor as described in the Appendix.

On 10 April 1895 Lowcock and Hill sold their newly-defined concession to the Electric & General Contract Corporation, but twelve days later the E&GCC sold its tramway interests and concessions for £39,000 to a new company, the General Traction Company, registered by Graff Baker on 20 March. The E&GCC retained only the Roundhay tramway, then about to close, and was finally wound up in 1904. The General Traction Company thus acquired the concession for the Marine Drive line, and proceeded to draw up plans and place orders with suppliers, mainly USA-based. The tramway was now intended to run from the entrance gates to the proposed 'pavilion and gardens' at Little Ness, and was to be completed and opened by 1 June 1896. Later extension to Port Soderick or to the Castletown Road was allowed for.

A separate company, Douglas Southern Electric Tramways Ltd, was incorporated on 21 October 1895 to own and operate the new tramway when built. Its capital was £50,000, divided into 30,000 7 per cent preference and 20,000 ordinary shares, and the registered office was at 17 King Street, Manchester (transferred in 1897 to Atlantic Chambers, Brazennose Street). Share allotment took place on 6 November 1895. Sir John Goldie-Taubman was chairman, and Dr Edward Hopkinson was consulting engineer. DSET were to pay the General Traction Co £29,000 for building the line, £17,070 in cash and £11,930 in shares (7,834 preference, 4,096 ordinary), this to cover a tramway from the entrance gates to Little Ness, a car shed and power station, cars and equipment, and three new bridges which, when erected, would become Marine Drive property. The General Traction Co could also contract for any extensions, at the rate of £9,500/mile. The DSET's first managing director was G.W. Lowcock; other early directors were W.P.J. Fawcus and J.S. Goldie-Taubman. T.J. Hutchinson and W. Davenport joined the company later, the latter remaining a director until his death in 1907.

In February 1896, the tramway concession was transferred to DSET and finalised at thirty years, with a payment to the Marine Drive company of one penny for each passenger (since each tramway ticket would also give access to the Drive) plus 5 per cent of the gross receipts. The 1d per passenger was in turn subject to a 2.5% of DHMD tolls payment to Sir John Goldie-Taubman, and was always separately accounted for. Construction of the Marine Drive tramway had meanwhile commenced (on 30 December 1895 or 13 January 1896 – sources differ), and by late February the chairman was able to report completion of roadbed and arrival of rails. By April, the depot had been built, the wooden bridges were being replaced by steel (Horse Leap had been done) and the power station was well ahead. W. Lavington Fletcher was resident engineer, assisted by G.C. Pritt, with J.T. and J. MacMahon for overhead, and Morris Owen of Heenan & Froude, the bridge contractors. Construction was supervised at first by W.S. Graff Baker.

At this distance in time it is still clearly to be seen how, to Graff Baker, the Douglas Southern project represented a once-in-a-lifetime opportunity to put electric traction right in the 'front window' of contemporary tourist development. The ready acceptance by the Manx Government of the innovatory Douglas and Laxey and (most recently) the Snaefell lines was in marked contrast to the mainland climate in these matters.

A change of control now occurred in the contracting group. In February 1896, Graff Baker sold his General Traction Company shareholding to a New York bank, and retired from the business shortly afterwards.

The premature <u>death</u> of W.S. Graff Baker on 1 June 1897 (he had been born in 1865) came to be recorded in 'The Blue Book' (a contemporary trades directory): this subsequently involved the Author in a variety of enquiries as in no British technical publication can his obituary be located. The Archivist of the Institution of Electrical Engineers was able to list Blue Book entries for the period 1890-98 and also provided copies of the records of Graff Baker's election to Associate and then to Membership of the IEE, whilst Mr Carey Graff Baker, his grandson, was able to furnish the material we illustrate (concerning 'The Lord Baltimore' electric car truck) and the 'dates' of the family members immediately of concern, together with an excellent portrait by an unknown artist (possibly painted at the time of his marriage in 1888).

Assembling all this information, we have the following outline of his U.K. activity for the period 1890 to early 1897 – as this is written a search of American newspaper sources is in hand in case something may emerge as to the cause of his untimely death.   His son (and namesake) 'W.S.G.Baker III' (to use American notation) would have been only about 8 years old at the time of his father's death. He too went on to ascend the engineering 'ladder', becoming Chief Mechanical Engineer to London Transport Railways.

(b. 1889, d. 1952).

Returning to W.S.Graff Baker (II), the following summarises his London based activity:

1890: Manager of the electric railway department of Laing, Wharton and Down at 82A Baker Street – 'L, W and D' were then Thomson Houston's UK agents.

1890-91: 'L, W and D' agency replaced by direct representation of Thomson Houston International Electric Co at 35, Parliament Street by W.S. Graff Baker, who concurrently became an Assoc. IEE.

1893: W.S. Graff Baker now also Manager of the 'Electric and General Contract Corporation' (essentially still his own business, it seems)

1895: Thomson Houston representation abandoned.

1896: W.S. Graff Baker occupied with the DSET, as in text. Transferred from Assoc. IEE to MIEE in April of that year. Still at 35 Parliament Street as 'Consulting Electric Traction Engineer'.

1897: Office now at 13, Austin Friars.

1898: Blue Book records his death aged 32, on 1/6/1897)

Concerning his Manx affairs, as already mentioned, late in the 'sixties Mr. O.S. Wrangham (then Agent to the Nunnery Estate) was able to allow the Author access to a remarkable cache of DHMD papers, including those left by Graff Baker himself. Particularly interesting was a hard bound exercise book, its dark red cover given gold tooled title lettering and containing Graff Baker's own manuscript account of much of the matters here discussed, plus correspondence from his London office (his letterhead revealed a telegraphic address of 'Giraffe, London'!). This material cannot now be traced.

When to all the foregoing is added his role as President and Treasurer of the Baltimore Car Wheel Company – and as its designer – it is obvious that his work load must have been a prodigious one. His elder brother John Paul Baker (1863-1947) was company secretary. The Baltimore Car Wheel Co was ultimately absorbed by Bemis (c. 1916).

Resuming, he purchasers formed an alliance with a syndicate about to build electric tramways at Norwich, and brought in two projected Philadelphia suburban tramways, later to form the Darby, Media &

Chester Street Railway. To manage this international tramway empire, a new company, New General Traction Co Ltd, was registered in London on 24 March 1896 with a nominal capital of £140,000 to take over the General Traction Co's interests, contracts and concessions; a major UK shareholder was Baron d'Erlanger, but the enterprise was American-inspired, and both the managing director (Edmund A. Hopkins) and the chief engineer (I. Everson Winslow, formerly the GT Co's secretary) were American citizens. Hopkins and Winslow joined the DSET board, and Winslow took charge of construction at both Douglas Head and Norwich; he later invented the internal spring trolley standard, which was used almost universally on open-top cars in this country.

One of the last acts of the General Traction Company before selling out to NGT was to obtain an agreement for extending the tramway to Port Soderick. The concession allowed for both this and a line inland along the Drive to the Castletown Road gates, but on 8 March 1896 Graff Baker wrote to Sir John Goldie-Taubman recommending that the line should go on to Port Soderick, the other branch being deferred. His advice was accepted, and the inland line was never built. The extension required an increase of £10,000 in the issued capital of DSET, and the final cost was £11,145, provided wholly by New General Traction through their nominee Alfred de Turckheim. The NGT holding in DSET was thus increased in 1897 by £5,573 in preference shares and £5,572 in ordinary shares, which gave them a controlling interest and made the DSET virtually an NGT subsidiary.

What of the line actually built? The single track, of 4ft 8½in in gauge, was laid on the landward side of the existing water-bound macadam carriage drive, which was widened where necessary, especially at the passing places. Leaving the loop at the Douglas terminus, the line curved round the Head, and almost at once the Drive assumed the form of a ledge cut in the cliff face; in the middle of this section was a small 'half bridge', later narrowed by removing the outermost girder (the parapet walls still betray this change). Immediately beyond stood the ornamental Drive entrance and toll-gate, prominently lettered 'Marine Drive 1891'. The line passed through the landward arch, and beyond was the second loop. About half a mile further the line reached the first major engineering feature, a three-span lattice-girder bridge 117ft long, carried on lattice piers and at first paralleled by the wooden bridge of 1891; this was dismantled about 1909 and its timbers used as additional supports for the newer bridge. This spot was known as Pigeon's Stream.

Immediately beyond the bridge was the power station, on the seaward side, and here also was the third loop. The small stream, of exceptionally good water, was contained within tanks and used to supply the boilers – indeed, the power station had to be situated here, because at no other point could the necessary water be obtained. The power station was a building of brick and stone roofed with corrugated iron; a date stone on the west gable was inscribed 'General Traction Company 1896' and originally surmounted by a clock. The octagonal chimney stack was of Peel bricks with a cast-iron top, and stood some 60ft high, about 27ft from the south-east end of the building. The engine room formed the basement, and the upper floor the boiler room, plus a workshop with its own engine and vertical boiler, a lathe, and a small rest room; a hydraulic wheel press was placed parallel with the boilers. Outside lay a blacksmith's shop and coal storage sheds, coal being brought during the winter by horse and cart, an extra horse being needed up the steep slope from Douglas harbour. A refreshment room was added after 1900 at the rear of the power station.

From this point, after a short downhill stretch traversing more open ground the line rose considerably, reaching 267ft above the sea. Beyond this first summit were the two greatest engineering features of the line, first Wallberry bridge and next the bridge at Horse Leap. Wallberry bridge had two spans, total length 256ft, and was on a down gradient of 1 in 16.01, with the two spans at an angle of 102 degrees to each other; the steelwork weighed about 102 tons. Drawings published in the '*The Engineer*' for October 1896 showed the track offset to landward, but in the event it was laid centrally; the designed static load was 100lb/ft². Horse Leap bridge had one span, 120ft in length, on a down gradient of 1 in 59.6 (drawings show 1 in 42). The two bridges were situated close together about one and a half miles from Douglas Head, and both crossed deep gullies in the cliff face, replacing DHMD's pitch pine structures. In 1909 and again in 1919-20 the bridge-work was strengthened, with considerable stiffening of the corner pillars of Wallberry's central support tower. The section as far as Wallberry was known as the 'Taubman' section of the Drive.

At Little Ness, about 1¾ miles from the Douglas terminus, a broad shelf of land lay to seaward. Here was constructed the car shed, a wood and corrugated iron building 93ft long and 40ft wide; by January 1897 it had been lengthened to 110ft. It had four tracks, two with pits for three-quarters of their final length, and access was at first by a traverser; a workshop and staff annexe 15ft square was provided at the north-east corner. Originally there was no loop at this point, the shed being half way along a single line section, with the depot branch crossing the drive. A more isolated position for a car shed can hardly be imagined, and the

The 'Electrical Review,' 'Railway World' and 'The Engineer' all gave prominence to the DSET in 1896-97. This 'Railway World' view of Pigeon's Stream under construction (issue for January, 1897) is typical. The 'Electrical Review' has a good view of Wallberry in the course of completion, and a contemporary (summer 1896) view of a partly assembled car on the Little Ness traverser: they must therefore have arrived via Keristal?

company's Victorian letterhead betrayed nothing of the real location of 'Tramway Depot, Marine Drive'. The downhill section from Wallberry ended before the car shed, and then began the climb to the highest point of the line. Beyond the original seventh loop (at the Whing) it included the steepest gradient yet – 142ft at 1 in 11.36 – which came just before the summit, where the line reached a height of 280ft above the sea, 13ft higher than at Wallberry. The ensuing descent included even steeper grades, with 130ft at 1 in 10.43, easing to 152ft at 1 in 12.66, but half way down, beyond the eighth loop at Rebog, there was a short uphill portion, followed by the ninth loop (at Coolebegad) and further downhill sections, partly at 1 in 16.44 and 1 in 18.66. Both Whing and Rebog

The Pigeon's Stream datestone. A 1949 photograph by the Author depicts it already pock-marked by local 'riflemen', but enabled this sketch to be prepared – including the superfluous dot after the date!
Author

included 45ft radius curves.* In this way the line wound around several bluffs, and about 2³/₄ miles from the Douglas Head terminus reached Keristal, the tenth loop, where for the 1896 season it ended.

The Drive now turned inland to end at gates on the Castletown road, where an imposing entrance like that at Douglas Head had originally been planned, but where in the event only a bungalow and a corrugated-iron office were built, as earlier housing the registered office of the Marine Drive company. A footpath continued along the coast to Port Soderick, which was otherwise accessible only by a glen winding down from Port Soderick station on the Isle of Man Railway.

Development here was by M. & T. Forrester and family (also former tenants of Laxey Glen) and a promenade was built in 1897, with a date stone inscribed 'Erected by M. & T. Forrester, 1897'.

An obituary of Thomas Forrester in the IoM Weekly Times of 9 December 1950 was headed 'Pioneer of the Visiting Industry' and continued:

'Mr. Thomas Henry Monteith Forrester, who with his brother Maurice came to the Island about 60 years ago, died on Saturday at Ballashamrock, Port Soderick. The Forrester brothers had in the course of the years seen the Island grow into one of the leading holiday resorts in the British Isles, and were intimately connected with the visiting industry all their lives.

'Mr. Thomas Forrester came to the Island as chef for the Castle Mona Hotel. Later he took the Glen Helen Hotel, and then he and his brother carried on a confectionery business in Strand Street in

---

*At Rebog the strata was a perennial source of problems; it consisting of a soft conglomerate-like mass of clay, sand and pebbles.

A contemporary half-tone of the Power Station and of Pigeon's Stream's twin bridges makes a poor reproduction. Mr D. G. Coakham thus kindly provided this exemplary line drawing in which may be discerned the datestone, the mini-bridges to the boiler room and workshop area and the elaborate timbering of the Marine Drive's earlier bridge, later to be demolished. The smaller sketch, adapted from one by Stan Basnett, shows the two Nuns' Chairs as visible from Pigeon's Stream. DHMD's car notice has but one! (The chairs were supposed pre-reformation places of punishment for erring Nuns).

a shop on which the entrance to the Strand Cinema is now built.*

'In 1889 the brothers took over the Port Soderick Hotel, extending the hotel premises, building a restaurant and concert hall and as the years went on they gradually bought up the whole of the creek and glen from head to head and as far inland as the railway station.

'In addition to buying Port Soderick, they became owners of the Fort Anne Hotel and Queen's Hotel and carried on a large cafe at the Pier Buildings. When their families grew up, the partnership between the brothers was dissolved. Mr. Thomas Forrester retired from active business just before the opening of the 2nd World War, and has lived quietly at Ballashamrock ever since. He was a very likeable man, and during his long life as a prominent citizen of Douglas made a host of friends'.

Our later illustration of the Port Soderick complex illustrates just what a thriving concern 'M & T' created – their landscaping activities

*Strand Cinema now demolished

ultimately embraced the whole length of the Glen.

To return to the story of the Douglas Southern, with the line complete to Keristal, an 'opening' ceremony was held on Thursday, 16 July 1896, though the line had not yet been inspected or passed! Three special motor cars carried an official party including Dr Edward Hopkinson and Marine Drive directors on a full inspection, following a luncheon at the Villiers hotel at which Advocate Kneen spoke of the possibility of a Spring Valley extension by an inland route back to Douglas. Refreshments at the power station and a speech by managing director G.W. Lowcock concluded the afternoon's events. Next day, 17 July, Major Cardew of the Board of Trade inspected the line for the governor, followed by Colonel Rich on 23 July, accompanied by the New General Traction Company's engineer, Mr. Winslow.

Rich reported on the 24 July. He found the curvature (the worst radius was '46' feet) and the gradients (to '1 in 9.1') severe. The bridges were of adequate strength, but he sought more fencing along the Drive generally 'to prevent persons, while looking at passing objects, from falling over the cliff'. He wanted the bridge decking covered with asphalt. Various special checks and fenders were suggested for the curve at the centre of Wallberry bridge, as were red and white signal posts at either end and at the termini, to assist the drivers in darkness or fog. His suggested speed limit was 8 mph. Pending the improvements his approbation was withheld.

Cardew had already reported on the 22nd. He found the American trolley collection system and the motor and control gear satisfactory, other

Director's special at Douglas Head, 16 July 1896. Standing in front of the car dash, and immediately behind (holding a child) are the brothers J. T. & J. McMahon. The trolley standard is of an early (experimental?) type, lacking the prominent external spring cluster fitted as 'standard' at an early (unrecorded) date. The NGTC car drawing mentioned in the text also features this mysterious early variant.

The late Mrs M. Marshall

When No 3 reached Little Ness, another 'photo call' gave us this interesting view of some of the major players in the Douglas Southern scenario. From left to right (as viewed) we have (third from left) W. Davenport, a 'disputed' figure (above whom is G. W. Lowcock in 'boater'), T. J. Hutchinson and, seated, I. Everson Winslow. With his hat in line with the corner pillar of the bulkhead is W. S. Graff Baker, and seated, again to the right, F. W. Saunderson of Douglas and Laxey Electric Tramway fame. The silk hatted are Marine Drive directors (the 'disputed person' is W. Lavington Fletcher or the DHMD's Emmott! . . . perhaps a descendant may recognise one or the other . . .).   *The late Mrs M. Marshall*

than in the complex manoeuvres needed to apply the electric brake (three handles had to be operated in turn, including the canopy switch) and sought (and obtained) warning notices at the Toll-Gates arch and insulation of upper-deck rails near the trolley standard. The bonding he approved.

These inspections, which were carried out under the Railway Regulation Amendment Act of that year, were preceded and followed by some hilarious correspondence between Rich, Lowcock and the governor's secretary, Storey.* The season was already advanced, and after further work had been done, the line was allowed to open for public service on 7 August 1896 'as far as the crossing place north of Whing Hill'. Press advertisements appeared from 10 August, and the fare of 1s return included either harbour steam ferry or swing-bridge toll at Douglas. On 5 September the modifications were complete and engineer James

---

*See Journal of the Manx Museum Vol VII, pp244-256.

Walker of the Harbour Board made his final inspection for the governor. The line being now acceptable, the letter of approval reached Manager Lynn on the morning of Monday 7 September, and the originally intended service at last began. The season ended on 26 September, 53,536 passengers to the good. For this shortened season, DHMD accepted a reduced toll of 2d per passenger.

Meanwhile, in 1895, the Marine Drive company had issued debentures to the value of £20,000 to finance the completion of the Drive (assumedly from Keristal to Port Soderick) on which the very last section of the tramway would be built. This outlay proved to be beyond the company's earning power (the tramway, when completed, took the lion's share of patronage), and by January 1899 the Drive concern was in receivership, a state of affairs which lasted until 1909. As mentioned earlier, the receiver and manager was Thomas J. Hutchinson, FIC, of Bury, and under his receivership a substantial surplus was accumulated.

During the winter of 1896-7, the tramway was extended by a total of three-quarters of a mile to the headland overlooking Port Soderick, now involving the embanking of the deep Keristal valley. One new and one relocated loop were involved, and reconstruction elsewhere reduced the maximum gradient; accounts differ as to details. From the terminus, a pathway led to the Port Soderick beach, some 180ft below; a separately-owned cliff lift was completed later, in 1898. The other lift at Douglas was added in 1900, both are described in the Appendix. The tramway was opened to Port Soderick on 1 April 1897, the start of the 1897 season. The DSET was always a seasonal operation, paralleled in Britain only by Snaefell and the Giant's Causeway line in Ulster.

The tramway staff consisted of a general manager, a car-shed foreman, and a traffic superintendent, all permanently employed, whilst engaged on a seasonal basis were an assistant car-shed foreman, three office workers (average), three inspectors, and (after about 1909) nine double car crews. On the generating side, there were permanently an engineer and assistant engineer, plus seasonal workers made up of two greasers, one foreman and a night watchman. The first manager was a Mr J.H. Lynn of Bradford, with USA experience, followed in apparently quick succession by a Mr Lynch. About 1899 there came another, former GT Co secretary F.W. Ketley, destined to stay until 1909. At the power station, the first engineer was a Mr Boulter, followed by Mr T. Ellison, then just before the turn of the century by Mr A. Randle, whose term of service lasted until 1930.

The single tramway track was laid with 65-lb rails, 30 feet in length, on steel sleepers at 3ft 6in centres placed on concrete 'cushions'; 100lb/yard rail was used on the bridges. Rail bonding was with 'Chicago' copper bonds. Points were of Marshall's patent spring type, both these and the rails being supplied by Alexander Penney & Co of London,* the points and crossings are unique in being guarded in street tramway style whilst being designed to mate with open Vignoles track. Some yet survive (off site) at the Crich Tramway Museum. Perhaps a set might one day return and be installed at a Marine Drive location by way of a memento. The

---

*A 107 Fenchurch Street address is all that is known of this concern

The aesthetically exceptional NGTC switchboard is prominent in this view of the western end of the Pigeon's Stream engine room, whose dynamos loom large in the foreground. The succeeding cross sectional view (looking N) explains the layout – the 'engines downstairs' arrangement allowed of solid foundations for the machinery but introduced a potentially damaging technical problem mentioned later in the text.   *Warburton, courtesy Manx National Heritage, and Railway World*

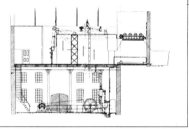

overhead was supplied by R.W. Blackwell & Sons Ltd, the poles (of bracket arm type throughout) being imported by them from the Morris Tasker Co of Philadelphia, USA. There were two types, of respectively 6in and 7in diameter. Double trolley wires were provided all along the line, the poles being placed on the landward side of both the Drive and the bridges. The No oooo braided copper overhead feeder was carried on the rear of the poles, and section gaps were spaced at about one-third of a mile. Major renewals were made to the overhead line poles in 1907 after trouble from corrosion, and the original ornamental brackets disappeared; the new galvanised top sections proved very durable and some of the poles have enjoyed a second life on the MER. The poles at Pigeon's Stream, Wallberry, Horse Leap, Little Ness, Whing, Rebog and Keristal

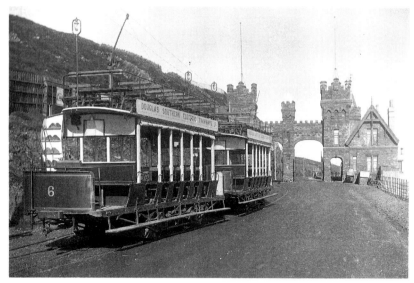

Virtually brand new No 6 and its trailer occupy the long loop just inside 'The
Gates'. The tower at the L of the twin arched gate had external stair access to its
single room(!), whilst a garden to seaward of the gatekeeper's house included a
somewhat vertiginous 'cabbage patch' at an angle of about 45 degrees, below which
yawned a cliff . . .   *Warburton, courtesy Manx National Heritage*

carried wood-mounted cast-iron nameplates, identical with those
formerly used for the majority of Douglas street names, those for
Wallberry and Horse Leap being at the bridge approaches. The overhead
line was originally supported by insulated ears mounted directly on the
bracket arms. Normal flexible suspension came later, probably in 1907.
    The generating equipment in the power station at Pigeon Stream
comprised two boilers, two engines and generators, and originally one
condenser. In the 50ft by 31ft boiler room on the upper floor, steam was
produced in two Babcock & Wilcox horizontal water-tube boilers of 4ft
5in diameter and 120lb/in^2 working pressure, with a heating surface of
1,426ft^2. They were fired by Bennis mechanical stokers of the natural
draught sprinkler type and were coupled to a Green's 96-tube economiser
working at 100lb/in^2. In the basement engine room, which was 50ft by 24ft
and 22ft high, were two Browett-Lindley 240-rpm horizontal engines with
steam-jacketed cylinders of 14in diameter and 14in stroke. These drove
through 17-in Eureka belts two Westinghouse six-pole 100-kW 550 volt
generators, running at 650rpm, the current from which passed to the
feeders through Westinghouse switchgear on white marble 'boards'. In the
separate pump room, 12ft below the engine-room floor, were two
Worthington boiler feed pumps, a Ledward circulating/air pump, and a
Ledward evaporative condenser cooled by seawater brought up by a third
Worthington pump. In 1898 the feed pumps and pump-room condenser
were replaced by two Ledward & Beckett condensing units with

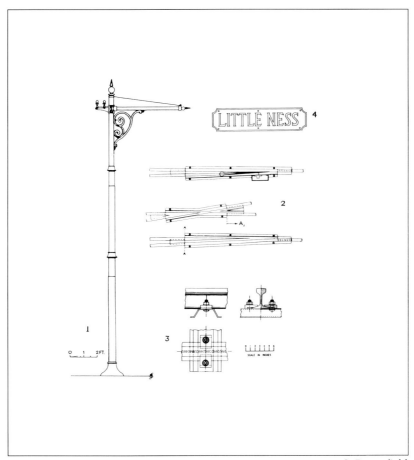

S. *Broomfield*

Some DSET elements . . .

1   A pole, bracket and bracket arm assembly, showing the pleasing design used. The original 'fixed' suspension ears were clamped to the bracket arm – as a trolley wheel approached it was found to administer a pronounced up and down flexing movement to the trolley wire which led to embrittlement near the ear: hence the later adoption of flexible suspension.

2   Alexander Penney's 'Marshall's Patent' pointwork. All the DSET pointwork, (apart from the depot turnout) consisted of equal divergence blades (in the outer rail) and fixed mates on the inner, with the same geometry applicable to both, obviously. The castings were cleverly formed, with extension pieces which fitted into the web of the three rails at their junction with the ends. A_1 to line A – A measured 28ft 6in. (Dwgs. 1 and 2 are to the same scale).

3   Detail of rail and sleeper and their fastenings. The outermost bolt lay $13^1/_2$ inches from the sleeper end, whilst the sleepers were positioned at 3ft 6in. centres. According to 'The Manxman' of 28 July 1896, each was laid on a concrete pad.

4   Surviving name plate from Little Ness. Among other items (now untraceable) was a cast iron plate proclaiming 'Alexander Penney & Co., Light Railway Engineers' which was found buried. It may well have been attached to the traverser.

Looking back towards Pigeon's Stream and the Gates.   *A. K. Kirby collection*

electrically-operated valves and motor-driven centrifugal pumps, and in 1906 the plant was augmented by an additional 72-tube Green's economiser unit. DSET was a determined 'moderniser' in seeking fuel economy.

The business office of the tramway, originally at the depot, was later combined with the ticket office at Douglas Head. Here, tickets could be bought at the rate of 1s return, 7d single, or about two-pence per mile. Tickets were checked on the car and at Port Soderick, and break of journey was allowed, a notice on the car bulkheads (from about 1906) suggesting places of particular interest. Another tiny 'office' existed at Port Soderick and, by 1910, to encourage pre-booking, a surcharge was levied on the cars, the single fare being 7d if paid at the ticket office but 9d if paid on the car. This move may have been coupled with a probable reduction from three-man to two-man crews for car and trailer. In 1900 a telephone line was installed from the Douglas Head office to the power station and to Little Ness car shed. There was also a permanent-way work-shop at Keristal junction, adjoining DHMD hutments.

Two further improvements prior to 1908 were the replacing of wooden fencing – which frequently blew away in winter – by iron, and the laying down of a proper car-shed fan at Little Ness, replacing the traverser. This probably used the points from Whing and Coolebegad loops, which were taken out, leaving nine loops. Seven of these were just long enough to take a two-car set, and were used as passing loops; the other, longer loops were at Port Soderick terminus and just inside the entrance gates on Douglas Head, the latter being used to store trailer cars on its seaward track, ready for use as traffic required. Operation of the line evolved to a

The tramway, as set in its most impressive surroundings at Wallberry.

Warburton, courtesy Manx National Heritage

Further to the south, this view of the Whing emphasises the narrow formation adopted south of Little Ness. The track appears as yet unused.
Warburton, courtesy Manx National Heritage

The nature of the narrower portions of the Drive is again well illustrated by this more modern view taken by Mr J. H. Price as car No 1 left the Drive on 23 June 1951 (just south of the Whing).

Another early view, again looking back (as is the earlier Whing illustration) is of a car and trailer seen against the 'crumbly cliffs' of Rebog. The lady in the foreground looks very pleased with herself, her companion apprehensive in the extreme . . . !   *A. K. Kirby collection*

pattern using fixed basic services of either four, five or seven cars, according to traffic requirements; these gave headways of 12-13 minutes, $10^{1}/_{2}$ minutes or $7^{1}/_{2}$ minutes respectively. Later, a six-car variant was introduced, and a system of oval head-code discs numbered 4, 5, 6 and 7 was adopted. Matching numbers were painted on poles at loops correspondingly scheduled as passing places, thus the maximum service was worked by seven cars, each showing a '7' disc and passing at those loops which bore a figure 7. The chief remaining problem was to inform staff of a change in service frequency with sufficient speed to avoid confusion, and there were some special variants of various shapes, including a number flanked by Maltese Cross symbols that may have been used when changing frequencies, and an 'LC' disc to denote the last car of the day. (See page 36 diagram).

This system of numbered discs may have been introduced as a result of a collision on Sunday, 4 July 1909, the only one known during forty-three years of operation. It was due to an unofficial motorman (actually a conductor) proceeding on to a single line section near Little Ness and meeting another car head-on. It occurred at 7pm, one of the cars involved being the last on service. The conductor received a broken ankle and his dismissal, and the proper driver was also discharged. Both cars were badly knocked about, but no one else was seriously hurt. In the same year, 1909, Mr F.W. Ketley took up the managership of the Norwich tramways (another NGT subsidiary) and was replaced on 31 March 1909 by Mr R. Orton, hitherto with the NGT-owned Coventry tramways. Mr Orton had already spent some time on the DSET in 1897, and was

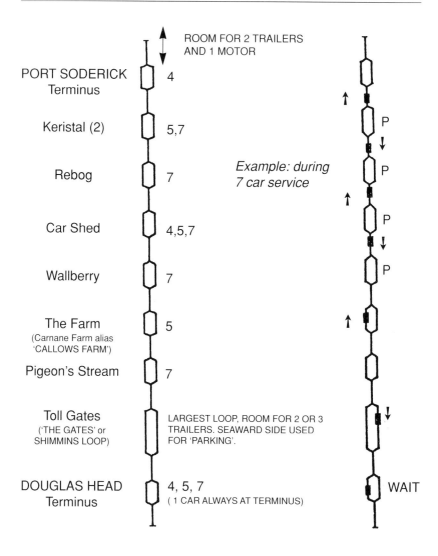

Operating system diagram for Douglas Southern tramway, using four, five or seven cars. The loops are numbered according to which service frequency used them. In the diagram on the right, P represents a passing place then used. The loop here named 'Car Shed' is that shown as Little Ness (2) on our track plan. Readers are invited to consider that needed for six cars (unrecorded!).

destined to retain the managership throughout the tramway's life; his recollections, in retirement, were of great value in preparing this account.

Douglas Southern Electric Tramways Ltd – Traffic Results

Year	Number of days' running	Mileage	Passengers carried	Gross Receipts	Receipts per car mile	Average cost per car mile
1898	132	40,963	94,173	not given	not given	not given
1899	133	37,593	100,769	not given	not given	not given
1902	137	32,505	192,031	£3,944	29.12d	14.84d
1903	123	32,344	201,280	4,135	30.68	16.23
1904	134	35,076	192,075	3,989	27.28	15.75
1905	114	33,313	210,298	4,055	30.66	16.52
1906	121	34,133	229,316	5,542	30.52	15.57
1907	125	36,666	231,664	5,613	36.74	17.69
1908	115	34,050	206,994	5,012	35.32	17.22
1909	125	36,570	194,826	4,790	31.43	14.67
1910	133	36,739	196,088	4,812	31.43	14.99
1911	118	34,578	230,653	4,422	30.69	15.97
1912	124	34,647	212,528	4,076	28.23	16.27

Year		Mileage	Passengers carried	Traffic Receipts	Total Expenses
1919	103	?	156,714	£7,714	£2,689
1920	130	32,421	267,671	13,539	5,738
1921	96	25,240	181,242	9,121	5,637

(*Courtesy of the late W.T. Lambden*)

An additional 5 per cent of the gross receipts became payable to the Marine Drive company from 1 November 1905; the DSET took this in its stride and by 1913 was paying the full 7 per cent dividend on its preference shares and 3$^1/_4$ per cent on the ordinary shares. But with the outbreak of war in August 1914 the summer season was quickly brought to an end (with only 112 days' operation) and for four anxious years the Marine Drive knew no tramway service (but some kind of special working in 1915 added 10s 8d to tramway tolls = 128 passengers) (DHMD balance sheet). Only 1$^1/_2$ per cent was paid on the preference shares for 1914, and in June 1916 the company was obliged to issue a mortgage debenture for £3,000 on its property. The Drive itself remained open, taking £50 in tolls in 1916-17.

The directors of the DSET throughout this period were T.J. Hutchinson (chairman), I.E. Winslow and E.A. Hopkins; the place left vacant by Davenport's death in 1907 was not filled. In 1919, Winslow moved to Barcelona, and J.G. Mills was appointed to serve while he was abroad. Mills resigned later in the year and was replaced by William Hart,

As early as August of 1896, a photographer depicted No 4 at the (incomplete) terminus on Douglas Head, the hut to the rear being the original tramway ticket office. Photographer Woodcock's substantial studio-showroom is also visible (he also occupied the older house to the rear, which still survives), and the railing about to be erected along the top of the DSET's embankment wall can be seen lying in the foreground. Notice the rigidly mounted suspension of the overhead line. No 4 sports the same trolley standard as No 3, seen previously.

Courtesy Manx National Heritage

succeeded in 1923 by W.F. Yaxley.

With the coming of 1919 work went ahead with preparations for reopening. Some strengthening was undertaken to the bridges, an additional Worthington boiler feed pump was installed, and the overhead wiring was renewed. A new workshop was built and equipped at a cost of £547 at the south-west corner of the boiler room, and the total cost of renewals in 1919-20 was £4,000. Thanks to the exceptionally good 1920 season, this was paid for out of revenue, the company's issued capital remaining at £41,445. Profits earned in subsequent years were £3,104 in 1922, £2,494 in 1923 and £2,089 in 1924, the company's financial year ending on 31 October.

Early in 1919, a serious breakdown occurred when condensate water forced off the cylinder head of one of the Browett-Lindley engines. The remaining undamaged unit had to maintain the power supply throughout the 1919 and 1920 seasons. A Bellis-Morcom 250kW compound set was then purchased and arrived in July 1921, being placed in service (after overhaul) in September. This engine and generator (Bellis & Morcom Ltd No 1466) was built originally in 1902 for Farnworth Corporation Tramways; its two totally enclosed vertical cylinders were of 15½in and 24in diameter, the stroke in each case being 12in. It was placed in a lean-to at the front of the power station, and took over the normal working, the

A glass slide provided this early view of shunting at Port Soderick. No 3 has pushed its trailer into the loop, and is (no doubt) about to move back so as to run round and couple up. Perhaps those on the top deck were making an immediate return? Also observe the wooden fencing which originally fenced the landward boundary of the Drive. That on exposed sections repeatedly blew away until replaced by iron. *A. D. Bailey*

Probably the choicest of the many entrance-to-the-Drive 'operational' photographs is this pleasing Edwardian example from the collection of A. K. Kirby.

This view of Port Soderick directs attention to the close proximity of the Isle of Man Railway (it next turns sharply inland to cross the Glen) and shows the variety of structures erected by the Forresters. The stone house 'buried' in the middle was the original hotel, reputedly erected by a sea captain returned from the Napoleonic wars. The two small 'trams' visible on the promenade are the bodies of the two-car Falcon Cliff lift, whose machinery came to function on the longer incline at Port Soderick.

Browett-Lindley engines (repairs having now been completed to the damaged unit) being kept as standby machines.

The new set had a nominal output of 250kW at 550 volts, working at 350 rpm, but at Farnworth it had been regularly worked at 300kW. The only major later modification to the steam generating plant occurred in 1926, when the Bennis stoking installation was converted to forced draught operation; new condensers were installed in 1929-30.

In 1921, an agreement was made with Douglas Head Marine Drive Co that, at the end of the concession in 1926, the two companies would be combined, the Drive company taking over the tramways. The amount paid to New General Traction for their interest has not been ascertained, but was clearly well below their original investment. In 1928, the NGT reduced its then capital by one-third and changed its name to the General Consolidated Investment Trust Ltd, in which form it still existed as late as 1970.

Douglas Southern Electric Tramways.

ENGINEER'S REPORT.

Date...*Sund July 4th*...1909.

General condition of Station ..*Good*..

Started No. 1 Engine............ .....a.m.   Voltage...............   Shut down...............p.m.

Started No. 2 Engine...*9.20*.....a.m.   Voltage.*500*.....   Shut down..*8.45*..p.m.

No. of Boilers.*No. 1*..........   Line test.*full*......AMPS.

Opened current on line........*9.30*.........a.m.   Shut down...*8.45*......p.m.

Average steam...*100*...... ..lbs.   Vacuum...*26*.......inches.

Temp. of feed water..*170°*   Temp. of feed tank ..*120°*   Temp. of engine room...*74°*

No. of Cars on line...*9*..   Trailers...............   Miles run..*269*...   State of rails....................

Engine oil used...*6*......pints   Cylinder oil used...*3*....pints   Dynamo oil used............pints
                                                                    -3712

Coal consumed *34*.... cwts.   Ashes drawn............ ...lbs.   Clinkers drawn...*192*..lbs.

Appearance of smoke emitted from chimney ..*Light*....   Condition of fires...*Good*....

Engineman on watch ....*C. Killey*..............*8*......a.m....*9*.....p.m.

Greaser   ,, ...*R. Kaslan*..............*-*......a.m....*-*....p.m.

Fireman   ,, ...*R. Kneale*...............*-*......a.m....*-*....p.m.

Watt Meter reading.........*52235*

Brought Forward.........*51916*

Kilo Watt Out-put To-day.........*.319*

REMARKS *A Collision occurred at about 7 p.m. To-night
at the point where Little new Loop used to be
through I Coin Driver running to Shut Instead of
Stopping at Farm Loop and the Fat Car Put one
running to Douglas Head with passengers. The persons
were Shoots & Harrison Conductor who was driving the Car from
past Soderich got His ankle..... A Randle*..............Engineer
Proper Driver A Shimmin   Broken Both Cars Badly Smashed

Thomas J. Hutchinson, chairman of DSET for most of its life, now
headed the combined undertaking. He had been responsible for the
rescue of the Marine Drive company from insolvency to its 1909
reconstruction, and looked on the Drive as a family concern just as the
MER had been the Greenwell's. The Douglas Southern's concession
ended on 3 April 1926 and cars Nos 1-12 acquired the new lettering
'Douglas Head Marine Drive Ltd'. The old DSET was not wound up until
15 April 1929, the delay being due to litigation arising from the death of a
workman who fell from Wallberry bridge (5 March 1927) while engaged
on bridge maintenance. Each winter, well-greased workmen (on danger
money) clambered about daubing the bridge structures with tar hot from
a wagon, leaving a visible coating of tar drippings across the rock far
below. This apart, no incidents involving injury to passengers or staff are
known, other than the 1909 collision already mentioned, and despite its
gradients, curves and cliff-edge location the tramway had an excellent
safety record, though the Board of Trade would have frowned on the
practice of greasing the curves around the Whing and Rebog.

DOUGLAS HEAD MARINE DRIVE ELECTRIC TRAMWAYS

Passengers may, on request to Conductor, alight from
and rejoin a Car at any stage en route which may be
of interest to themselves.

PLACES OF PARTICULAR INTEREST.

PIGEON'S STREAM (View of NUN'S CHAIR)   .   REBOG
WALLBERRY   .   TheWHING   .   KERISTAL.

DHMD car notice (20in x 10in) which came to be fitted over the RH bulkhead
window, obscuring the original fleet number. It seems likely that these notices had
a DSET predecessor (see comments in text on post 1909 number exchange by 3 and
11). The LH position was occupied by a framed and glazed notice exhorting
passengers to pre-purchase their tickets at the terminal offices. Note the incorrect
'Nun's Chair' reference (see p. 25 illustration).

Author's collection

The tramway take-over introduced an unusual complication to the DHMD
accounts, arising from the need to account separately for that part of the
tram fare which represented the Marine Drive toll and for the percentage
of gross tramway receipts paid over in return for the concession. To avoid
undue disruption to the accounting system, DHMD each year produced
separate 'tramways department' accounts as part of their balance sheet,
the 'tramway commission' and tolls being shown as though the line was
still under separate management. By 1929, the DHMD had a debenture
debt of £4,500, part representing a payment of 1926 to DSET for half the
post-1918 bridge improvements and the rest arising from the take-over.

Results after 1929 were less good, and in February 1931 a second
debenture issue of £6,500 to T.J.Hutchinson became necessary.
Competition began to make itself felt; this competition was indirect, for

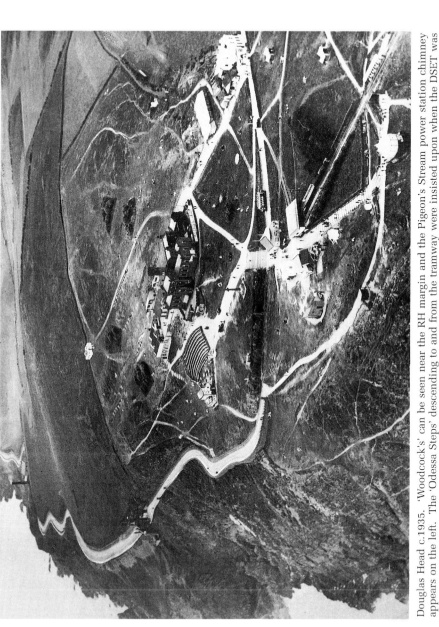

Douglas Head c.1935. 'Woodcock's' can be seen near the RH margin and the Pigeon's Stream power station chimney appears on the left. The 'Odessa Steps' descending to and from the tramway were insisted upon when the DSET was constructed as 'necessary' to retain public rights of way (the concrete footpath provided to the Gates also arose from this agreement). The verandahed building is the DSET/Marine Drive office, which functioned chiefly in the former connection, as only turnstiles and gatekeepers were needed to control non-tramcar Drive admissions. A car stands on the terminal loop.

The late R. Orton

motor coaches were not allowed on the Marine Drive, only private motor vehicles being given this privilege. The annual general meeting in 1930 heard of a profit of only £596; tramway earnings had been £5,084, with wages at £750 and car repairs at £55. The sum of £210 had been spent on engines and boilers and £254 on condensers, with the result that the tramway had lost £94 on the year despite a passenger figure of around 101,600. Mr Randle left in 1930, his place as engineer being taken by a Mr Foxon, engaged seasonally.

In May 1932, the DHMD tried hard to obtain permission to run charabancs into Douglas and compete for traffic there, but narrowly failed to obtain the town council's approval. Instead, a ticket office was opened on the Victoria Pier, Douglas, and a ticket introduced giving travel to Port Soderick via the harbour ferry boat, Douglas Head Incline Rly, Marine Drive tramway and Port Soderick cliff lift, at an inclusive charge. In about 1936 the ordinary fares were dropped to 1s 6d return, 10d single, with an evening excursion at 1s after 6pm. The cars received electric headlights, to allow for later running in the evenings.

Because the depot was so isolated, a car was left overnight at Toll Gates loop, minus controller keys, for staff transport next morning; this car always carried a barrel of fresh water to Little Ness depot. When the service commenced, two cars went together straight through to the Head, and another followed, waiting at Wallberry for the first service car. Thereafter, a car was always standing at Douglas Head loop to tempt potential riders. Two-car sets were slow and the speedier single cars frequently had to wait at the loops when both were running.

In 1935 a public supply at 3,300 volts three-phase AC, 50 cycles, was brought to two 125kW Hewittic Electric Co Ltd rectifiers installed in the power station, with separate 196-kVA oil-immersed rectifier transformers by the Hackbridge Cable Co. Maximum demand was about 160kW. Operating from May 1937, the season's consumption was 43,405 units. The cars were now noticeably more lively when running.

In the now-silent power station, the small workshop which originally had a small engine and vertical boiler now relied on an electric motor for power, while downstairs the 1896 switchgear passed the supply from the nearby rectifiers to the overhead. The steam plant was broken up during the winter of 1936-7, though the boilers and stokers remained in position until 1938, when they were sold and removed to Greece for further service. In 1938 and 1939 the power station served as a garage for two blue-painted 15/16-seater Morris charabancs which were hired to collect late passengers after the cars had stopped running. At Keristal, the café proprietor would ring a substantial ship's bell (engraved Douglas Head Marine Drive Ltd) five minutes before the last car left for Douglas.

The annual general meeting in June 1938 covered the first year of operation from rectified public supply. Tramway earnings had been £4,609, wages £1,741 (Drive and trams) and passengers 92,174, but the profit at £722 was again disappointing. Abandonment of the power plant wrote off £4,705 (against £409 from sales) and the company's indebtedness had again risen. The book value of the line remained high (£19,369), reflecting DSET auditors' criticisms over the years of inadequate provision for depreciation. No dividend was paid, and the concern was in fact 'just holding its head above water'. Efforts to improve appearances had seen £55 spent on new uniforms.

Power consumed in 1938 was 40,275 units, while in 1939 it amounted to 37,130. The line ran for the last time on Friday 15 September 1939, the power being disconnected next day. The final year of operation (to 31 March 1940) saw the gate takings and 1d toll per tramway passenger total £470 as against 1938's £581. The company's wage bill had been £1,645 – the actual tramway passenger figure and earnings are unknown. The directors were W. Townley Cottam (secretary), Percy Hutchinson and James Downs Hutchinson.

On 23 May 1940, Cottam wrote to the Nunnery agent stating 'We have decided not to run the Tramway during the War, and I regret the inability to anticipate any future situation. If there are any passengers, however, the customary toll will be due and payable...'

Little remains to be added. The Royal Navy, taking possession of Douglas Head, sealed off that end of the Drive and ultimately demolished the ticket office, whilst Port Soderick fell into a decaying slumber from which it did not recover until 1963-4. On 12 September 1942 the rectifier installation was removed, leaving only the 3,300-volt line to show the source of power supply. In 1946 the Marine Drive company's Receiver disposed of the whole property to the Isle of Man Highway and Transport Board, who found that the bridges would require complete reconstruction. Meanwhile the Marine Drive company was finally dissolved on 12 January 1948, and the site of the Drive, stripped in 1946-7 of track and overhead, then relapsed into the solitude it knew prior to its opening in 1891. Between 1948 and 1956 the Drive was variously 'closed' and 'open' to pedestrians.

The purely road scheme ultimately evolved was to cut back into the rock at Wallberry and Horse Leap, thus by-passing these two bridges, whilst at Pigeon's Stream an embankment took the place of the bridge and obliterated the remains of the power station. A new approach road was built right down to Port Soderick. The task took from 1956 to 1963, and cost £240,000 (£60,000 a mile).

In 1963 battery-electric passenger vehicles operated by the MER board were proposed (together with a chairlift across Douglas harbour) and vehicle trials were held, but the finally chosen scheme was the operation of conventional motor buses (along with private vehicles). Although experiments were made with the intention of allowing two way bus operation, the service was in fact to be a uni-directional one, from Douglas southwards.

As work on the Drive began, Douglas Corporation elected to purchase Port Soderick and embarked on a total reconstruction, the facilities now including a dance hall as well as bars and restaurant/cafe provision (the Corporation already had many years experience in managing the much larger Villa Marina complex in Douglas – a lunch coincident with the 1976 horse tramway centenary was well appreciated by a wide range of guests, and typified Douglas civic hospitality and its professional competence). The Glen to the rear was now the site of a very large car

Two informal crew snapshots dating from the 'thirties: No 4 seems to be at 'The Farm' loop, whilst No 2 features the headlight(s) fitted c.1936.
The late R. Orton and Tom Cowley

park, to which the reconstructed (and diverted) southern extremity of the Drive had direct access. Douglas had a long established tradition of operating certain out-of-town bus services in which vehicles were lettered 'extended area' (as the initials, EA) their licences permitting this operation. The bargain which seems to have been struck with the Isle of Man Road Services gave the latter the actual Marine Drive route to operate, but the Corporation ran under 'EA' rules from the town up the old Castletown Road and in at the 'Keristal' entrance. Double deck vehicles turned at the car park, but smaller buses actually turned right down at the 'promenade'.

In 1966, when the Drive had been (re) opened for three years, problems with the new formation and underlying (and overhanging) strata, particularly at the critical sections at Wallberry and Horse Leap, began to show themselves.* At the southern end of the site of Horse Leap bridge the DHMD's rock shelf had been considerably widened, in large part by tipped material, and sea erosion soon began to eat at the base of this embanked material. Equally, the geological disturbances resulting from the major blasting operations seemed to have become an ongoing phenomenon (typically, the removal of protective overburden admitted water to strata hitherto kept dry, initiating annual frost damage to the near vertical bedding planes of the rock). A first precautionary closure of the outer lane was followed by withdrawal of the 'bus service. Then, finally, the road was effectively severed, only a footway remaining. For a few years this too experienced closure, the footpath over the cliff tops first

*See also Mr Basnett's text.

Alec B. Quayle, the IMRS traffic manager looks on as buses JMN 936 and LMN 546 pass at the northern approach to the site of the DSET's 'Rebog' loop. This showed two-way working to be possible on the rebuilt Drive, but services were in fact only operated 'N to S'. The date is 'early' in the short lived renaissance of the Drive (i.e. the mid 'sixties).   *Stan Basnett*

provided in the middle '50's (to avoid crossing the bridges, whose planking had progressively disappeared) being re-established on a new route, appreciably further inland in terms of the original geography. The situation had stabilised again by c.1980, the footpath along the inside of the driveway being re-opened. A turning place for vehicles just short of Wallberry provided for tourist's cars – at the opposite end of the Drive the road was closed north of Keristal until 1995, when it re-opened to Little Ness.

The Corporation was faced with diminished patronage at Port Soderick as the 1970s wore on and the operation closed after the 1980 season (the loss of the Drive as scenic approach no doubt played its part). Corporation works in 1985-6 saw the emergence of a Sports Centre type complex. By 1993 other owners attempted a Marine sports centre operation centering on diving and similar pastimes. However, in 1996 the premises are now 'the Anchor' a public house with function room and appropriate catering. The severed (in vehicular terms) Drive remains a forlorn monument to 'modernisation' (its chief protagonist happily failed in his crusade to substitute its 'road vehicle technology' for the Manx Electric and Snaefell operations!).

Rolling Stock

The original fleet consisted of twelve double-deck cars, Nos 1-6 being motor cars and Nos 7-12 trailers. A prototype drawing was prepared by the Brush Electrical Engineering Co of Loughborough in October 1895, showing an unusual car on a Peckham truck. A more accurate general-

The two principal sources of 'deliberate' DHMD tramway photographs are the views taken by the late B. Y. Williams in 1934 and by W. A. Camwell in 1939. Colour versions of two of the latter appear in our colour section, and include the 'point of departure' on Douglas Head, already featured in earlier views (the Entrance Gates and Pigeon's Stream are also well represented previously). Of the balance of the Williams/Camwell grouping, here are

Top left: No 2 against the rock wall just N of the Wallberry bridge. Note the 'Pantasote' blinds *Author's collection (via the late B. Y. Williams)*

Top right: B. Y. Williams' view of an informal moment at Keristal – the fresh water can may relate to the absence of a water supply at Little Ness shed.
Author's collection

Bottom left; B. Y. Williams' view of No 4 northbound on the Keristal–Port Soderick section, where the wider road of 1896-97 is a conspicuous feature. Apart from Port Soderick terminus we have no other views of this section.
Author's collection

Above: W. A. Camwell's classic view of No 5 poised on Wallberry: 30 May 1939.
National Tramway Museum.
Below: W. A. Camwell's view of Nos 8 and 13 outside the car shed, 30 May 1939.
National Tramway Museum

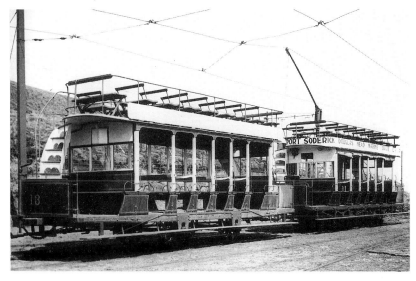

arrangement drawing bears the General Traction Co title and is dated 2 May 1896. Apart from their equipment, all twelve cars were of identical design. They were double-deck, open-top, open-ended cars, with cross-bench seating and open sides to the lower deck, including seats on the outward sides of the bulkheads, under the short canopies. Seating was for seventy-five persons, thirty-nine on the upper deck and thirty-six on the lower. On each car both stairways faced the same side, as the roadway was always on the seaward side of the line; the trolley standard was on the landward side of the top deck, instead of in the centre. Similar but diametrically opposite situations applied at Guernsey and on the Swansea and Mumbles line.

The dimensions of the cars were: wheel base, 6ft 6in, length, 28ft 4in (29ft 5in with couplings), maximum width, 7ft 4in, and height to top of trolley standard, 14ft 4in. Built by the Brush Electrical Engineering Co Ltd, Loughborough (the enamel builders' plates showed the former title of Falcon Engine & Car Works), the trucks were imported from the USA. These were of the then new 'Lord Baltimore' type, designed by W.S. Graff Baker and made by the Baltimore Car Wheel Company of Baltimore, Maryland. The two motors in cars Nos 1-6 were of the Westinghouse 12A type, of 25 horsepower, and the controllers were Westinghouse type 28A. The motor cars weighed about 6 tons 6 cwt, the trailers 3 tons 13 cwt.

Two features of the Lord Baltimore truck deserve special mention. One is the elaborate spring platform assembly from which the motors hung – almost centre of gravity suspension was achieved. Another was the inclusion (on the Douglas Southern) of truck trusses very similar to those familiar on Peckham trucks used by Sheffield in the present century. They were cleverly tailored to fit around the truck itself and were a Baltimore Car Wheel Co. design, presumably Graff Baker's own.

In 1897, four trailers, Nos 13-16, were delivered by the Brush Co, generally similar to the 1896 cars but mounted on lightweight horse-car type trunnion running gear, again of 6ft 6in wheelbase. The weight was only 2 tons 12 cwt, and seating was for seventy-six, the extra seat occupying the space which on the 1896 trailers had a platform base for a trolley standard, so allowing the latter cars to be converted to motor cars if desired. Accordingly, two, Nos 7 and 8, were thus converted in 1897 (GE records state 1898); two General Electric 800B 27-hp motors were fitted in their 'Lord Baltimore' trucks, and General Electric K 2 nine-notch controllers were added. Any of the Nos 9-12 batch could have been so motored, and after the 1909 collision Nos 3 and 11 exchanged identities, the motor truck and equipment from No 3 going to the erstwhile No 11, which was renumbered 3 (except for its internal bulkhead numbers, by now hidden behind route notices!)

The livery was crimson and white, lined out in gold and white, with trucks in black and rails etc in brown. This continued until about 1933, except for the post 1926 change in the title carried on the upper deck sides of cars Nos 1-12 (on Nos 13-16 the DSET title was simply painted out). In 1933-4, the paint style was simplified to yellow lining on crimson, but the more elaborate gold with white parallelling line survived on several trailers. End decency panels lettered 'Port Soderick' were added to the motor cars and some trailers by 1907-8.

Other modifications over the years concerned the side blinds and the lighting. As delivered, the cars had simple canvas blinds with equal red-and-white vertical stripes and leather retaining straps to secure them when fully rolled or lowered. On the landward side, whose boarding step was in fact never used, the cars had a waist-level barrier rail on vertical guide irons, as on Blackpool and Fleetwood car No 2 at the Crich Tramway Museum. After 1909, cars Nos 1, 2, 3 and later 6 were given a waist panel on the landward side, with the footstep removed, and these cars then received on that side differentially-striped draw curtains arranged in three parts, fastening back to the first, third and fifth pillars and supported by brass rails. The seaward side openings received Peters' patent blinds of 'Pantasote' cloth, running in mouldings attached to the pillars; these could only be lowered to seat level. In the late 'thirties, these 'Panasote' blinds were replaced by full-length canvas rolled blinds much as of 1896 design, with a leather strap and brass buckle fastening them to the car sill; possibly they were taken from trailers Nos 13-16.

The electric lighting consisted initially of three ceiling lights downstairs and two tall standard lights upstairs, one at each stairhead. There were no headlights, but oil-lamps were originally carried in the lowerdeck bulkheads; the trailers had oil lighting only. The stairhead lights had been removed by the 'twenties (or earlier) and two ceiling lights under the canopies took their place. The oil lamp lamphouses had gone from the motor cars by the 'thirties, and when the electric headlights of c.1936 appeared their power source may have been the line voltage with 2 x 250v bulbs in series? (the wiring did not survive the BTC's restoration and the lamps were stolen at Little Ness). The motor cars originally had experimental spirally sprung trolley masts, but after 1900 these were replaced by outside sprung standards by R.W. Blackwell & Co. Plug and socket centre couplings were fitted to all the cars.

Although there were a hydraulic wheel press and a substantial lathe in the power station, the occasional 'flats' were dealt with by fitting carborundum-faced brake shoes to the car affected. No cutter (of conventional steels) will machine chilled iron treads or flanges: they are 'glass hard'. All cars ran with chilled iron wheels throughout their lives, with large flange profiles; there were no grooved rails on the tramway , and although the points were guarded in street tramway fashion, they had large grooves. A tower wagon and flat truck, both hand propelled (or horse-drawn?) were provided for maintenance purposes.

After closure, the final distribution at Little Ness, (entrance doors to rear) was Nos 1, 4, 2 and 11 on the seaward road, Nos 3, 5, 6 and 8 on the next, Nos 7, 15, 9 and 10 on the third road and Nos 12, 16, 13 and 14 on that to landward.

In 1950, the Highway Board donated a car and trailer to the Light Railway Transport League's Museum Committee. Efforts to remove one car proved 'difficult', so the trailer rescue, was, sadly, abandoned.

The story of surviving car No 1 from 1951 onwards involves successive 'homes' and its ultimate rating by The National Museum of Science and Industry as one of a select group of exhibits now deliberately retained in

A 1950s shot of the last two poles, with forlorn suspension ears still in evidence on the bracket arm of that nearer the camera. 'Tram scrapping' of the era often used this low-cost method of removing the trolley wire.   *Author*

Pigeon's Stream bridge and power station c.1953.   *J. N. Slater*

its 'as first preserved' condition. When on 23 June 1951 the Museum Committee of the Light Railway Transport League removed No 1 to storage at the Quarter Bridge yard of the Highway and Transport Board, it expended a substantial sum (in terms of its then budget) but was in fact treated very generously by the Board in view of the costs actually incurred. The 'saga' of the journey included traversing a newly tarred and chipping-surfaced section of the old Castletown Road which removed the solid tyres of first the front, then the rear, axle of the horse car transporter borrowed for the move from Douglas Corporation. Frequent oiling of the latter's smoking brass bearings continued throughout the entire journey, the car getting under the Kewaigue railway bridge with 2" to spare, just as an afternoon IMR train headed south over the same arch. Later, opposite the then HQ of the IOM Electricity Board, the contact pressure of the small and narrow-treaded front wheels saw a twin tarmac 'bow wave' develop until the axle bit into the road. Much jacking and a 150 yard journey on planks overcame this further impasse. It was early evening when the car finally came to rest at the Quarter Bridge – we had left Little Ness late in the morning!

By the end of 1955, intended developments at Quarter Bridge made the storage site no longer available (the car had been 'tented' over a wooden framework before winter of 1951 arrived) and the LRTL Committee still lacked a Museum Site. Thus the vehicle was offered to, and accepted by, the late John H Scholes, Curator of Historical Relics to the British Transport Commission. Shipped from Douglas aboard IoM Steam Packet Co 'SS Peveril' on 20 March 1956, an ensuing repaint at Charlton works overseen by the late Richard Elliot drew attention (in the process) to the excellent physical condition of the vehicle. When the BTC's Clapham museum opened it made an attractive exhibit, but went back into

The 'landscape seen from the sea'. Launches had plied to Port Soderick from early in the century, and a post war resumption enabled the late Tom Cowley to secure this unique shot of Wallberry. What a spectacle late evening cars must have presented.

Horse Leap bridge – a box camera study by the Author (c.1949-50) seems to be its only visual perpetuation as a structure in its own right.

Left: 21 April 1956: a view of the collapsed remnants of Pigeon's Stream bridge. This scene followed the explosion of demolition charges, and was succeeded by a similar demolition of the shell of the power station, all then being buried under a culverted embankment and a new car park.   *Stan Basnett*
Right: Next, 1958: following the Island's own 'big bang', somewhere under this enormous mass of rock debris lie the remains of the Wallberry viaduct. A solitary pole still stands sentinel . . .   *Stan Basnett*

'hibernation' when Clapham closed in 1974. Its ownership then passed to the Department of Education and Science.

It became part of the Science Museum reserve collection and in March 1975 came to be loaned to the Tramway Museum, (now National Tramway Museum) at Crich, Derbyshire. When the late Mrs O.E. Kelly of Peel (a daughter of Reginald Orton) visited Crich in late summer of 1975, she and Mr. Kelly were given an upper deck ride on Car No 1. The car ran quite well on normal track, but climbed on the rear of its oversize (USA standard) flanges when passing through conventional street tramway pointwork.

For this reason, regular Crich operation was out of the question. A next excursion on 12 July 1980 was destined to be its last under power, when the late W.A. Camwell was able to photograph the car with his customary expertise for the first time since his famous series of views of 1939. The revised policy now adopted by The National Museum of Science and Industry already referred to means that there was no question of the car operating on the Island in 1996 (an aim which had interested Isle of Man Railways as part of their ongoing programme of railway attractions). The Author had other (family) commitments on 12 July 1980, but listened with interest to a recording made at Crich that day – the car ran so quietly that the motor hum was barely audible above the conversation of its (on this occasion) exclusively lower deck passengers.

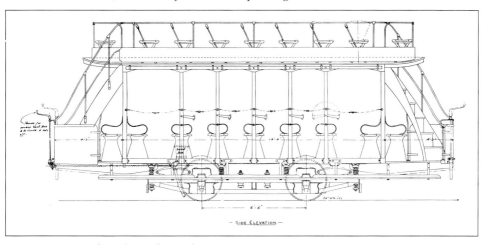

A view taken from the early prototype drawing for a Douglas Southern car mentioned in the text – note the Peckham truck. *Isle of Man Highway and Transport Board (1951)*

Falcon Engine and Car Works plate, black on white enamel (3^1/$_2$in by 1^5/$_8$in).
J. C. Cooke from photo original

DSET car No 1 with its 1909 body modifications.   *P. Hammond*

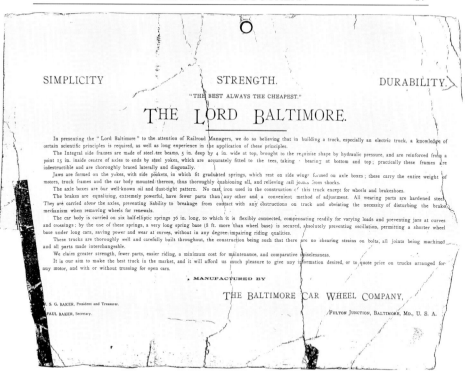

SIMPLICITY   STRENGTH.   DURABILITY.

"THE BEST ALWAYS THE CHEAPEST."

THE LORD BALTIMORE.

In presenting the " Lord Baltimore " to the attention of Railroad Managers, we do so believing that in building a truck, especially an electric truck, a knowledge of certain scientific principles is required, as well as long experience in the application of these principles.

The Integral side frames are made of steel tee beams, 5 in. deep by 4 in. wide at top, brought to the requisite shape by hydraulic pressure, and are reinforced from a point 15 in. inside centre of axles to ends by steel yokes, which are accurately fitted to the tees, taking · bearing at bottom and top ; practically these frames are indestructible and are thoroughly braced laterally and diagonally.

Jaws are formed on the yokes, with side pockets, in which fit graduated springs, which rest on side wings formed on axle boxes ; these carry the entire weight of motors, truck frames and the car body mounted thereon, thus thoroughly cushioning all, and relieving rail joints from shocks.

The axle boxes are our well-known oil and dust-tight pattern. No cast iron used in the construction of this truck except for wheels and brakeshoes.

The brakes are equalizing, extremely powerful, have fewer parts than any other and a convenient method of adjustment. All wearing parts are hardened steel. They are carried *above* the axles, preventing liability to breakage from contact with any obstructions on track and obviating the necessity of disturbing the brake mechanism when removing wheels for renewals.

The car body is carried on six half-elliptic springs 36 in. long, to which it is flexibly connected, compensating readily for varying loads and preventing jars at curves and crossings ; by the use of these springs, a very long spring base (8 ft. more than wheel base) is secured, absolutely preventing oscillation, permitting a shorter wheel base under long cars, saving power and wear at curves, without in any degree impairing riding qualities.

These trucks are thoroughly well and carefully built throughout, the construction being such that there are no shearing strains on bolts, all joints being machined and all parts made interchangeable.

We claim greater strength, fewer parts, easier riding, a minimum cost for maintenance, and comparative noiselessness.

It is our aim to make the best truck in the market, and it will afford us much pleasure to give any information desired, or to quote price on trucks arranged for any motor, and with or without trussing for open cars.

, MANUFACTURED BY

THE BALTIMORE CAR WHEEL COMPANY,

W. S. G. BAKER, President and Treasurer.

PAUL BAKER, Secretary.

FULTON JUNCTION, BALTIMORE, MD., U. S. A.

Above: Advertisement card (of 1896) for the Lord Baltimore truck, including the names of Graff Baker and J. Paul Baker as principals of the Baltimore Car Wheel Company. The notes on W. S. G. Baker in the text indicate that he spent much time in this country after 1890, and (from the above) his 'hats' also included being responsible for the more technical aspects of the Baltimore company's activity in the area of truck design.   *Carey Graff Baker*

Below: The motor suspension of a Lord Baltimore truck, as arranged for the 12A motor. No 7 & 8s G.E. motors fitted less easily, needing special ropework to allow of armature changes.

           Trade press, 1896

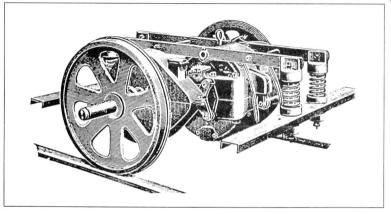

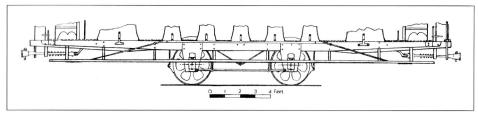

The underframe and running gear of a lightweight trailer.   *Author*

(contd. from p.55)

Efforts by the Author to remedy several deficiencies on the car have included the manufacture of a set of curtains for the landward side, but as delivered these had several dimensional and manufacturing errors and will require correction (tentative arrangements are being made). More readily replaced are the missing gongs and starting bells. The BTC were sent a pair of the latter, but these were lost 'somewhere' – happily another survived in the Author's possession and another has been found (of the same type) in Douglas Corporation's 'dump', albeit damaged. These items should reach Crich by summer of '96! American friends have supplied parts which will enable restoration of the 'Pantasote' blinds to the seaward side. Obviously, Science Museum approval for these restoration 'additions' is being obtained at each stage. (Vandals had destroyed the originals).

Other 'Marine Drive' tramway relics are a curious mixture of accidental survivals, some from the papers held by the late Reginald Orton, others from material which had found its way into the possession of the Highway Board. Some bridgework drawings, a number of large scale blueprints of the Lord Baltimore truck, and a (sadly discoloured) colour drawing of a car and trailer are typical (the latter includes some errors). There is also a Morris Tasker pole drawing and one from Alexander Penney's of a standard point. All these found their way to the collection of the Manx Museum, along with the 1895 Brush prototype drawing already mentioned.

The reuse of DSET poles by the MER has been a successful piece of 'salvage' (they are of course shortened appreciably). In the late 50's some DSET rails were laid just north of Halfway House (the Author went to look!) but their rust pitted heads made their traverse very noisy and only these two lengths (4 rails) were laid (and later removed). As mentioned earlier, the depot track fan was removed to the Crich Tramway Museum (in 1960). The depot, and the remaining fifteen cars,were broken up where they stood in the winter of 1951-52.

Fleet List – Douglas Southern Electric Tramways

Car	Motors (2)	Controllers	Truck	Body	Seats	Date
1-6	Westinghouse 12A, 25 hp	Westinghouse 28A	'Lord Baltimore'	Brush	75	1896
7-8	General Electric 800B, 27 hp	General Electric K2	'Lord Baltimore'	Brush	75	1896
9-12	nil (trailers)	nil	'Lord Baltimore'	Brush	75	1896
13-16	nil (trailers)	nil	Brush Trunnions	Brush	76	1897

Nos 7 and 8 were built as trailers in 1896 and motorised in 1897-8.
Nos 3 and 11 exchanged numbers, trucks and equipment in 1909.

Mid-morning on Saturday 23 June 1951: the Author and Mr W. E. Vick discuss the impending removal operation (R) whilst volunteers make a final check of the upper deck stowage of the trolley standard.   *D. W. K. Jones*

Moving day progresses . . . (i) No 1 reaches the end of the depot track   *D.W.K. Jones*

(ii)   A close-up of tramcar 'levitation' in progress. The gap between ramp rails and trailer rails was of the order of 1.5" – the observant volunteer to the right seemed little concerned for his own safety (whilst the Author experienced considerable trepidation in <u>his</u> role as brakesman!).
                              D.W.K. Jones

(iii)   The load looms large over the front wheels of the horse tramcar transporter as the (somewhat heavier!) bulk of No 1 is secured.   *J. H. Price*

(iv)   A halt during the descent from the Whing, whilst the second Aveling Barford dumper is coupled up to function as a brake (Another shot captured the car at Keristal, just as it left the tramway route – the then Café proprietor rang the Marine Drive Co. bell by way of farewell as the convoy moved on !).   *Author*

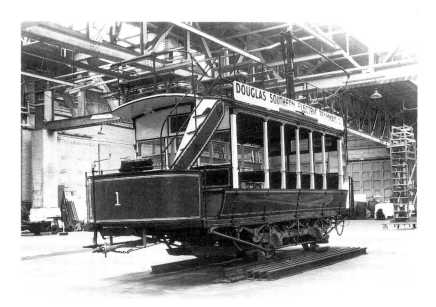

This view of No 1 at Clapham shows the excellence of the BTC's repaint and also the stiffening trusses mentioned in the Baltimore Car Wheel Company advertisement. The constituent members must be assumed to be in compression (and were probably tubular), hence their obviously larger diameter than orthodox above-floor truss rods, which are of course in tension and normally lie concealed in the body panelling of a saloon tramcar. Extraordinarily, when the DSET cars received their side panels an above-floor truss rod (of the tensioned variety) was added at the 'waisted' side of the cars concerned! *The late R. Elliott*

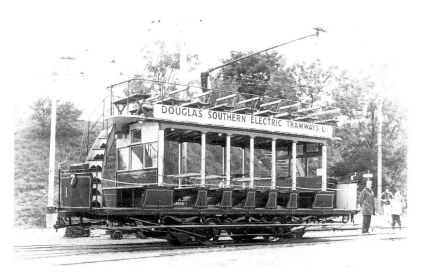

On 12 July 1980 the late W. A. Camwell was able to renew his acquaintances with DSET/DHMD's No 1, as ever producing a classic photograph.
National Tramway Museum

Tickets of the Marine Drive tramway

The late W.H. Bett kindly provided the notes which follow, along with (loaned) tickets from which the black and white illustrations to which his text refers were prepared. By way of update we include some further examples in the colour section. Also included are Mr. Bett's notes on tickets from the two cliff lifts, with one illustration, again in black and white. As a tailpiece, there is also reproduced the advertisement side of a horse tramway ticket of 1968, featuring the Corporation's No 15 'bus service (5).

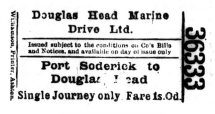

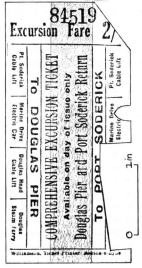

Four of W. H. Bett's specimen tickets relating to the Douglas Southern Electric Tramway. The numbers relate to the text concerned. Three other specimens (from the Author's collection) appear in our colour illustrations section and are of 1930s origin. The fifth ticket is mentioned above.

About 1899 DSET used railway-type Edmondsons, bearing no printer's name, dated in a press and in horizontal two-coupon form for returns. These included Douglas Head to Port Soderick single, brown; Port Soderick to Douglas Head single, primrose(1), adult return left-half blue, right-half pink; child return left-half white, right-half green. Both the above returns have the Port Soderick – Douglas Head half on the right.

By the 'thirties, tickets were roll issues by Williamson, of normal bell-punch size. These included single Douglas Head to Port Soderick, green (1s 3d); single Port Soderick to Douglas Head, yellow (1s)(2) (later reduced to 10d); 6d single covering either Douglas Head – Little Ness or Little Ness – Port Soderick, in either direction, grey; all the way adult return, lilac, 2s (later reduced to 1s 6d); half-fare return, blue (1s). In 1938 there was also an evening excursion return (lilac with red stripe) for 1s; and for 2s a combined (day) excursion ticket (4) from Douglas to Port Soderick beach and back, including 'Douglas Steam Ferry' 'Douglas Head Cable Lift', 'Marine Drive Electric Car', and the 'Port Soderick Cable Lift' down at the other end. This, illustrated, was buff with a red stripe. Some sections were apparently cut out, the operators retaining the clippings as vouchers to be produced when claiming their share of the proceeds.

Cable Inclines and the Ramsey Pier Tramway
By the 'twenties, the Douglas Head incline railway followed the practice, not uncommon on funiculars, of having returns and no singles. Upon collection of (nominally single) fares at the turnstiles a roll ticket by Williamson was issued, bearing no fare but worded 'this ticket is available for RETURN journey FREE on day of issue only'. The title of the line and a heading 'RETURN TICKET' also appeared; and across one end, the day of the week. Colours were changed daily; a Tuesday issue in pinkish buff (3) and a Thursday issue in bright green with blue stripe, are typical. They were torn in two on the return journey.

The Port Soderick Holiday Beach Lift's tickets by 1938 were of Automaticket machine type (but apparently issued manually, as all seen are roughly torn off). They were 1d white, and 2d blue, headed 'Port Soderick Holiday Beach' on the face with the fare on each half; on the reverse the word 'LIFT' appeared diagonally across each half together with some fancy decoration.

An advertisement card (5in x 3in, on green card) from Port Soderick, dating back to the turn of the century. The reverse side lists meals (at mouthwatering prices!) and mentions the exclusive use of produce from the Forrester's two farms (and of 'fresh daily' bakery products from their Douglas establishments).

TRAVEL FACILITIES AND FARES

CAR AND BUS SERVICE.

WEEKDAYS .. 10.0 a.m. to 9.0 p.m. (or later*)
SUNDAYS .. 2.0 p.m. to 9.0 p.m. (or later*)

ONE TICKET INSTEAD OF FOUR

SPECIAL.—Two Shilling "4-in-1"
Tourist Return Ticket, Douglas Pier
to Port Soderick via The Marine
Drive, covering Steam Ferry,
Douglas Head Cable Lift, Marine
Drive Electric Car and Port
Soderick Cable Lift Fares: obtainable
at the Ticket Office outside Victoria
Pier Cafe. Children half price.
THE "4-IN-1" TICKET MEANS
A SAVING OF 5d. PER PERSON
on the ORDINARY RETURN FARES
Get your ticket and then board the
Steam Ferry Boat with the Red
Funnel.

ELECTRIC CAR FARES

DOUGLAS HEAD TO PORT SODERICK
Via The Marine Drive.

RETURN TICKET 1/6
SINGLE TICKET .. .. 10d.

EVENING EXCURSIONS
(Commencing July 1st)

From 4.0 p.m. to 9.0 p.m.
(or later*) Daily.
RETURN TICKET 1/–
Book at Tramway Office, Douglas
Head. Cars every few minutes.
*According to demand.

DAILY POST PRINTERS, LIVERPOOL.

THE MOST POPULAR Half-day EXCURSION

Too Good to Miss

PORT SODERICK ON THE DOUGLAS HEAD MARINE DRIVE TRAMWAY

An advertising leaflet (6¹/₄in by 7in when opened out) printed on a primrose paper and obviously dating from 1938-39 (hence the 'buses reference).

A.D. Bailey collection

DOUGLAS HEAD MARINE DRIVE

THE Marine Drive extends from Douglas Head to Port Soderick, a distance of 3¾ miles. Average width in the rock cuttings, 30 feet. A carriage-road branches from the Drive at the KERISTAL SIGNPOST to join the Castletown Road to Douglas ; this circular route is under 6 miles.

There are two entrance gates ; one at Douglas Head, the other near the Castletown Road adjoining Oakhill. The terminus is at the cliff head above PORT SODERICK.

For the convenience of visitors, the Company has provided a considerable number of seats at suitable points along the Drive. Light refreshments are obtainable at LITTLE NESS, half-way to PORT SODERICK.

THE ELECTRIC TRAMWAY

THE trip to PORT SODERICK by the Electric Tram is an inexpensive pleasure which all who appreciate marine scenery will greatly enjoy. Starting from DOUGLAS HEAD we pass in turn such places of Manx traditional interest as Pigeon Cove and the NUN'S CHAIR ; we then traverse the 250 feet span across the precipice at WALLBERRY and the shorter steel bridge at the HORSE LEAP, 300 feet above sea level, from which a long, sweeping curve is made to LITTLE NESS Promontory. The many "corners" and sinuous windings of the track sustain our interest in the varied and quick changing road scenes. The abrupt transitions from the broad expanse of wild vegetation on the slopes of Little Ness to the towering bare cliffs of the yoke-shaped WHING and thence to the buttressed wall of brown-yellow clay at REBOG are especially noteworthy. At Rebog the road is but a SHELF 'TWIXT SEA AND SKY, but when KERISTAL BEND is rounded, widens appreciably towards its terminus, 100 feet above the most popular little seaside resort, PORT SODERICK.

On previous page: An excursion handbill of 1938-9 date (8³/₄in x 5⁵/₈in, the printing black on pale blue). The Author has a fire damaged <u>evening</u> excursion leaflet printed in black on salmon which advertises essentially the same bargain but may have carried a lesser fare of (1s 6d?) in view of the shorter stay possible at Port Soderick). *A. D. Bailey collection*

William Sebastian Graff Baker 'II', c.1888. His son bore the same names, hence is styled 'III', his father (obviously) being W. S. G. Baker (I). In W. S. G. Baker III's obituary, the elder Baker is referred to as having been involved in electric 'street railways' in the United States, so that all three practised in the same technology, consecutively. *Carey Graff Baker*

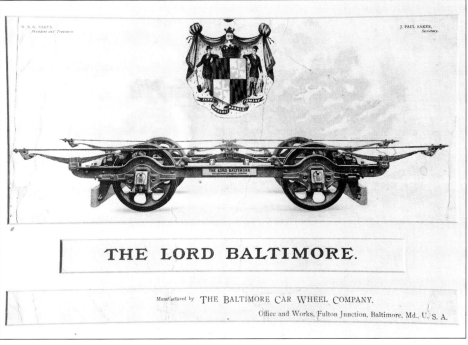

This delightful colour representation of the Lord Baltimore truck is crowned by a strange piece of 'heraldry' – the motto, in Italian, reading 'to do is masculine, to talk is feminine' (!). The RH supporter seems to be a lady 'fisherman,' complete with fish and rather dashing boots, the LH could be Graff Baker in person, complete with spade! Very whimsical . . . *Carey Graff Baker*

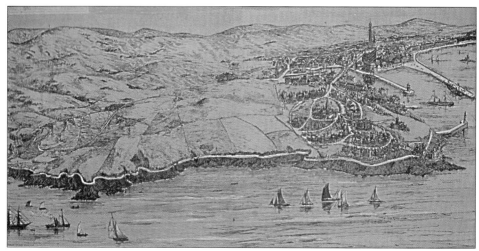

Reprise . . . The Marine Drive as depicted in 1890, with the (circular) Tower, a 'Gothick' estate, suspension bridges and an alleged length of six miles! *The late S.H. Davenport*

"SPECIAL PHOTOGRAVURE ART" Series
of Postcards.
12 VIEWS
PICTURING THE BEAUTIFUL COAST SCENERY
FROM DOUGLAS HEAD TO PORT SODERICK.

PUBLISHED BY
The Douglas Southern Electric Tramways, Ltd
ISLE of MAN.

DSET and the Marine Drive Co. both sold sets of cards – one of the better ones was a sepia set of 12 sold under the DSET imprint, of which this one of the Whing (featuring T. J. Hutchinson as a bystander) is a choice example. It is included in our colour section so as to do justice to its sepia tones, along with a reduced image of the containing envelope. *R. Orton*

The postcard featured here was on sale at Port Soderick in the summer of 1945, and was at once the source of an insatiable 'Douglas Head tramway' curiosity on the part of the Author. Exceptionally, it features Horse Leap bridge, and although its rock faces are a trifle pale, is quite a reasonable representation of the Marine Drive scene.
Author's collection

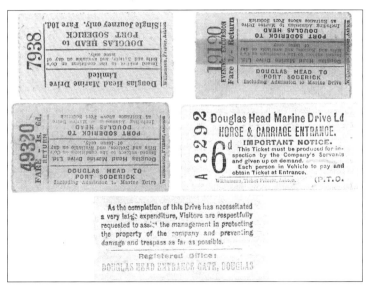

A group of latter-day DHMD Ltd tickets, excepting that for the 'Horse and Carriage Entrance' which appears likely to be of an older series which only sold slowly. The reverse (illustrated) carries wording which suggests perpetuation of a 'nineties format. The 'registered office' may never have been changed after its migration (date unknown) from the Castletown Road entrance to 'The Gates'? 'Latterly' (certainly from 1926) year-round manning was available at the DSET office building on the Head. All the other tickets advertise 'Hotel Port Soderick' on the reverse. *Author's collection*

The talents of Mr Stanley Letts provide this colour version of one of the famous W. A. Camwell views, in which two cars (7 and 1, and Inspector Colquitt) wait for passengers on 30 May, 1939 (Location Douglas Head).

Another Stanley Letts/ W. A. Camwell 'colour' shot shows No 1 waiting at Rebog, as seen from No 7 (30 May, 1939).

This colour photograph depicts the 1980 'excursion' by No 1 at the National Tramway Museum and was destined to record an electrical 'swan song', as it is no longer allowable for the vehicle to move under power. The transparency reproduced was taken on 12 July and is by Mr Terry Daniel (the Author hopes this is the correct attribution!)

DOUGLAS HOUSE OF KEYS

This attractive card (whilst tramless) clearly shows the separation of the tracks just opposite the one time Bank of Mona, by 1896 part of the Legislative Buildings complex which includes the House of Keys. *Author's collection*

JACOB'S CREAM CRACKERS THE VERY BEST

JACOB'S

Loch Promenade. Douglas, I.O.M.

A glimpse of the elusive No 68 comes as part of this pleasant postcard view, probably of pre 1914 date. *R. J. S. Wiseman collection*

Dave Menzies hard at work 're-trucking' No 72/73, immediately before 9 August, 1976. The 'midnight oil burning' came to extend to 5a.m.

DCC Group photographer

Almost 'ready to roll'. The late Duggie Sanderson (in white overalls) gave valued help in the final week of preparation, as did a host of others, including honeymooners Whiteley (Morning of 9 August). DCC Group photographer

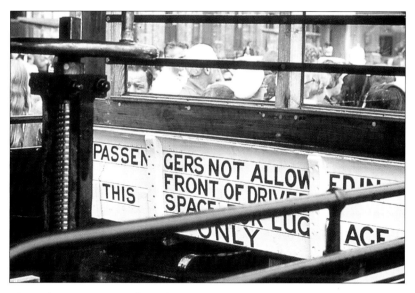

The underseat notice on the end seats, restricting their use (restoration by G. K. Whiteley and family).   *DCC Group photographer*

A 1977 view with a full load awaiting departure from the Victoria Pier's terminal spur (last used by 72/73 in 1993). The lifeguards were still not complete, and today yet lack their 'upper lips'.   *Author*

'Electrified' for 1995 – 72/73 at Victoria Street, having arrived without external propulsion, following Derek Shepherd's motorisation of that year (in which Isle of Man Railways workshop staff played a major role).

Chapter 3
The Upper Douglas Cable Tramway

Introductory note:

The actual construction of the Upper Douglas Cable Tramway had its origins in the 'entanglement' into which Alexander Bruce and his Isle of Man Tramways and Electric Power Company came to be drawn following the IoMT&EP's purchase of the Douglas Bay horse tramway in May of 1894* (the tramways concession from the Douglas Town Commissioners had but three more years to run). The horse care line was the <u>essential</u> feeder of the new Douglas and Laxey Electric Tramway, and although obtained relatively cheaply (£38,000) its possible take over (or re-leasing to others) by the local authority from 1897 was an obvious source of anxiety to Bruce and his associates.

The ensuing sketch of events is partly repeated in more detailed terms in succeeding text, but is here judged necessary in order to help 'set the scene'. This is also the point to emphasize the concurrent anxiety of IoMT&EP to electrify the horse tramway, so that their cars could connect directly with the steamers at the Victoria Pier, or, perhaps, be fed by smaller electric cars more suited to the promenade service. In any case, the promenade tramway in its 'present' state was a substantial money earner in its own right. Destined to remain unelectrified, in 1899 its year's passenger total attained 1.5 million.

Bruce's attempts at securing an electrified Bay tramway were to finally grind to a halt on 22 November 1897, following a concerted attack by 'car proprietors' (i.e. the owners of equestrian taxis) and their friends (and even kinsfolk) among promenade frontagers. A 20th century parallel might be seen in the early abandonment of an excellent horse tramway terminal station opened at the Victoria Pier in 1961!

Returning to 1894, Bruce continued to press the Commissioners for permission to electrify the Bay line (and to retain its operation after 1897), being now aware that the town, on its part, were desperately anxious to have 'someone' construct an Upper Douglas tramway. An excursion early in 1895 to the Streatham Hill cable tramway (a Dick, Kerr equipped line) by a combined IoMT&EP/Commissioners party indicates how matters were developing. Later in 1895 matters accelerated, under pressure from the hapless residents of Upper Douglas and also (in part) as a result of the impending change from the authority of Town Commissioners to that of a fully fledged Borough.

An Act of Tynwald came to be passed in November 1895, followed by an amending Act in May 1896 (when substantial portions of the cable tramway were already under construction, or even completed): heroic efforts by Dick, Kerr saw the line commence service by 15 August.

With this sketch in the mind of the reader, it is now time to more fully detail this colourful piece of late Victorian transport history.

'No pushee–no pullee–allee samee go like hell'
(unknown Chinaman, apropos San Francisco cable cars, 1873)

As implied in the above introduction, by the end of 1893, the Bay tramway had caused a definite shift in the pattern of local trade, affecting the business of boarding-house and shop owners in the inland upper

---

*(By now the property of Isle of Man Tramways Ltd., to whom it had been sold by 1882's purchasers W.D. Pitt, F.W. Barnett and G.J. Cuddon).

town, the late Regency part of Douglas that slopes up steeply to some 160ft above the bay. It had been suggested that the commissioners should lay a tramway to Upper Douglas, serving the older district, and lease it to the new consolidated tramway company.* At the first of several public meetings on 19 January 1894, the ratepayers of Ward 3, the worst affected area, pressed for a resolution 'that facilities be given for a tramway right round Peel Road and all the intermediate streets off Bucks Road,**which had not facilities compared to the front'. A Mr. T. Kelly pointed out that two bus companies serving the upper part of the town had failed, but despite this a deputation was appointed to demand from the commissioners a proper tram service to Upper Douglas. In view of the gradients, any such tramway would clearly have to use some form of mechanical power.

In January 1894, the Press revealed that the town commissioners had received two offers to lease the Bay tramway from 6 December 1897, when their right to purchase it took effect. One was from Alexander Bruce, chairman of the electric tramway company, the other from H.H. Crippen, later associated with Falcon Cliff. Crippen's offer included penny fares throughout the year, and he announced a public meeting for 5 February. He proposed to convert the Bay line to Dick, Kerr & Co's cable tramway system, for which he held a local concession. His penny fares bombshell upset the current negotiations with the electric company, by then advanced to such finite details as the rail section to be used on the promenade after electrification. Bruce withdrew his offer (by 27 January), and Crippen then did likewise. It later emerged that Crippen was a Derby Castle shareholder, and had tried to get a penny fare promise from Bruce in return for withdrawing his rival bid, his chief object being more grist for his own mill.

Crippen's meeting of 5 February was taken over half-way by two of the three town commissioners present, and ended with yet another plea for a tramway to Upper Douglas, Crippen's original resolution being amended accordingly. Its chief advocate was baker R.D. Cowin, a popular and thoughtful town commissioner, and its opponent was commissioner Edmund Chadwick, a determined conservative in the most negative sense. The next few months saw the issue twisted at times into 'upper versus lower town'.

An Upper Douglas Tramway Committee was formed, and met on 9 April 1894, to good effect; the Improvement Committee of the town commissioners recommended on 18 April 'that it is desirable in the general interests of the town that a system of tramway communication should be laid down between the lower and upper levels of Douglas'. They recommended that the data on hand should be properly tabulated and a report prepared by the town surveyor.

Surveyor Taylor reported in July 1894 to the effect that while the line would be a burden on the rates, it would also be an immense boon. A route via Victoria Street, Prospect Hill, Bucks Road and Woodbourne Road to Murray's Road, thence by Glen Falcon Road to Broadway was

---

*Who were currently about to acquire the Bay horse tramway.
** Bucks (plural) referring to gambling Regency expatriates who had retired there from Bath and Brighton (for example).

suggested. From the various alternative forms of traction, Taylor put forward two proposals; one was for an electric conduit line with single track and loops, costing £18,790, the other for a cable line estimated to cost £25,000. Either would be likely to lose some £1,500 a year. Electrification of the horse line on the conduit system and its joint operation with the Upper Douglas line was envisaged. The report was pigeon-holed, and by December a newspaper was criticising the commissioners for having set aside this subsidised tramway scheme until the town was safely through other undertakings already in hand.

Meanwhile, Bruce had sensed better things ahead, and (as earlier) reopened his discussions with the Isle of Man Tramways for the purchase of the horse line, achieving this by May 1894. He now renewed his negotiations with the commissioners for the <u>continued</u> ownership and future electrification of the horse line, whilst several of the commissioners, for their part, realised that this could be the means of securing a tramway for Upper Douglas.

Early in 1895, Bruce, Farrell, Callow and Aldworth of the Isle of Man Tramways & Electric Power Co and town commissioners R.D. Cowin and J.A. Brown travelled to London to visit the Streatham Hill cable tramway and were sufficiently impressed for Bruce to accept Dick, Kerr & Co as the builder of any future Upper Douglas tramway. They had already had considerable experience of cable traction, having taken over from the original Patent Cable Tramways Syndicate that stemmed from the San Francisco lines. Their initial surveys and drawings were to be prepared by June 1895 and bargaining with the town commissioners continued. The impending obsolescence of Streatham Hill obviously remained unperceived by Bruce and his party, and despite the presence of their own electric railway and events on the Marine Drive.

Meanwhile, a public meeting in Tynwald Street school on 21 January 1895 reviewed the lack of progress over the past year. In Upper Douglas annual rents of £40 had been reduced to £25, but still people were being brought to court for non-payment. Ward 3 and parts of Wards 4, 5 and 6 were equally affected. R.D. Cowin's speech placed the whole matter in a larger perspective, making the point that the lucrative Bay line should help to carry the cost of the cable line instead of imposing a betterment rate on those served. Opponents, led by Chadwick, still resisted any action, but public opinion forced their hand, and by February the committee appointed to look into the issue recommended that the commissioners should lay down the proposed line and lease it for twenty-one years to any company that would undertake to work it, the first four years to be free of any rental. They disliked Bruce's continuing wish to link the construction of the cable line with a lease of the Bay line. By 19 February, the commissioners had agreed to meet a further deputation from Upper Douglas, and the clerk was instructed to approach the directors of the tramway company and arrange a meeting.

Four weeks later, Bruce made a definite move. On 27 March, an IoMT&EP meeting at Mather & Platt's Manchester office passed a resolution which offered both the construction of a tramway to Upper Douglas and free electric lighting of the entire promenade and Victoria

Street, in return for a new lease of the Bay tramway for twenty-one years from 1897, authority to electrify and double the Bay line throughout, to supply electric power for general use, and to extend their tramway to the railway station. Dr. Hopkinson had reported on the technical aspects. The commissioners were offered 10 per cent of the Bay line's receipts, as rental. Although the recent Upper Douglas Tramway petition had received the signatures of over half the relevant ratepayers, the commissioners side-stepped most of the issues and in reply merely suggested a new lease of the Bay line at a minimum of £3,000 a year.

Still determined, Bruce offered to meet the town commissioners. Bruce, Callow and Farrell were invited to meet the improvement committee on 30 May 1895, and in return for a new twenty-one-year lease of the Bay line and power to double the remaining portions of single track, offered to build an Upper Douglas cable tramway and provide an interim bus service to Upper Douglas, pay the commissioners 15 per cent of the receipts of the Bay line, remove the horse-car sheds (but not the station) at Burnt Mill Hill, and to build a replacing shed at Derby Castle themselves! The bus service would run every ten minutes from Whitsun to October and every twenty minutes in winter. On 10 June the company (now really anxious) wrote again to the commissioners to say that even if the cable tramway were not built, they would run a guaranteed horse-bus service in Upper Douglas for 1895, 1896 and 1897 in return for permission to double the horse-car track, and on 14 June they offered to remove the rest of the horse-tramway buildings at Burnt Mill Hill (this is now Summer Hill).

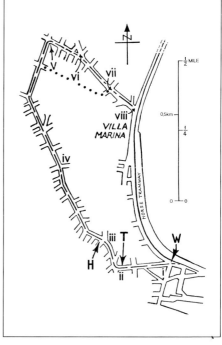

By the end of June, the commissioners had decided to accept the company's offer of 30 May and join with them in promoting a Bill in Tynwald, later to become the Upper Douglas Tramway Act, 1895. Since all parties were now anxious to have a cable tramway working by Whitsun 1896, Tynwald on 10 July suspended its standing orders to allow a special committee to examine the application at once. The committee comprised Deemster Gill (as chairman), the Attorney-General, J.R. Cowell, J.T. Cowell and J.T. Goldsmith. Messrs G. A. Ring, Kneen and Brown appeared for the company.

At the hearing on 16 July a joint petition by commissioners

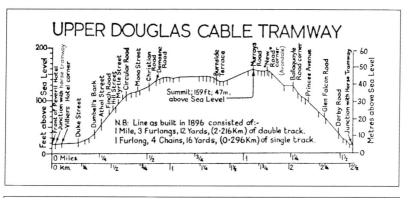

UPPER DOUGLAS CABLE TRAMWAY

N.B: Line as built in 1896 consisted of:-
1 Mile, 3 Furlongs, 12 Yards, (2·216 Km.) of double track.
1 Furlong, 4 Chains, 16 Yards, (0·296 Km.) of single track.

Summit; 159 ft; 47m, above Sea Level

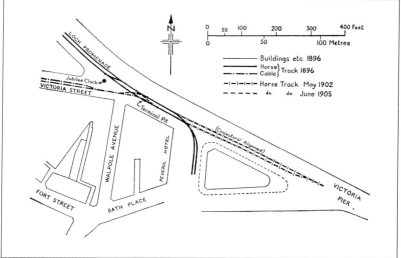

Buildings etc. 1896
Horse) Track 1896
Cable)
Horse Track May 1902
do. do. June 1905

and company was read, after which plans were produced and witnesses heard. The consulting engineer, James More, Assoc Inst C E, who had had thirteen years' experience of tramway construction, revealed that he had drawn out his plans in a mere three weeks, by dint of spending two 'on the ground' from 5am to dusk. He proposed three-rail double track with shared centre rail on 130ft of Prospect Hill (from Dumbell's bank to Athol Street) and for 240ft to seaward of Glen Falcon Road on Broadway, with double track elsewhere. The cars were to be 5ft 6in wide, and the maximum gradient 1 in 10.6. Other witnesses were William Mackenzie of Toronto, and W.H. Andrews of the

An outline of the cable tramway route. The tramway successively traversed Victoria Street (i to ii), Prospect Hill (ii to iii), Bucks Road (iii to iv), Woodbourne Road (iv to v), York Road (v to vi), Ballaquayle Road (vi to vii) and Broadway (vii to viii). Other related streets are Walpole Avenue (W), Thomas Street (T) and Hill Street (H). The earlier suggested route using Glen Falcon Road (via Murray's Road) is shown in dotted line. The Gradient Profile given relates to the above, whilst the smaller plan details horse and cable tramway terminal arrangements at the pier.

All J. C. Cooke

London Tramways Company, whose Streatham cable line had by then carried 9-10 millions a year on 2³/₄ route miles against 75 millions on 21 miles of horse-car line. The London cable cars had a much lower accident rate than the horse cars, and could stop in less than their own length. George Flett, director and joint manager of Dick, Kerr & Co, was able to point to 120 miles of tramway then built by his firm, and stated that Newcastle also proposed to have a cable line.

For the commissioners, clerk Nesbitt revealed that they looked on the bus service (introduced on 20 July) as a <u>separate</u> reciprocal bargain for the double horse car line from the Iron Pier to Castle Terrace. Commissioners J.A. Brown and S.R. Keig added favourable comment: Keig lived on Prospect Hill, whose widening would overcome an earlier objection by Edmund Chadwick that on the double track only 4ft 6in would separate a car from the kerb. Witnesses R.D. Cowin and Robert Archer described their losses in running buses in Upper Douglas, attributing them to the public's refusal to ride up the steep Prospect Hill on seeing the equestrian effort involved.

The opposition now spoke. Chadwick's recapitulation of past offers and negotiations was brought to an end by the Attorney General, and his financial doubts were countered by Keig quoting several instances of lines built as a social necessity in the full knowledge that they would be unprofitable. Alexander Gill, a builder, fared even worse (and seems to have been associated with the drivers of other conveyances who would lose business to the tramway). The findings of the committee were to be presented to Tynwald on 23 July if no further objections were received, and on that date they duly gained acceptance.

The report restated the agreement, adding a new clause to the effect that after seven years the cable line should pay 5 per cent of its gross receipts to the town. The committee agreed that it was mechanically practical, that Prospect Hill needed widening in any case, that the line was needed, and that the agreement was a fair one. The resulting indenture between the commissioners and the company on 15 October 1895, specified a minimum £1,500 annual payment for the Bay tramway and required the bus service to run daily (except Sunday) from 8am to 11pm between 1 May and 30 September, and from 8.30am to 10.30pm in winter. All this was subject to the Act being obtained within twelve months.

The Bill was read a first time in the Legislative Council by 3 August, and the Act was passed on 8 November as the Upper Douglas Tramway Act, 1895. After dealing with the Bay tramway, it specified that the new tramway was to be worked by wires, ropes, cables or chains, and fixed engines, and stated that:

> ... the tramway shall commence at a point forming a junction with the Douglas Bay tramway at or near the Peveril hotel.... thence pass the Jubilee Clock up Victoria Street, to a point opposite the offices of Dumbell's Banking Company Limited, thence up Prospect Hill, Buck's [sic] Road, Woodbourne Road, past the top of Murray's road to the next road beyond (ie, York Road of today – Author), down the last-mentioned road into Ballaquayle road and down the same and through Broadway to a junction with the Douglas Bay tramway at a point thereon about fifty feet south of the south building line

of Broadway, and such tramway so far as the same is a double line – that is to say, from the junction near the Peveril hotel to the road above Murray's Road – shall as far as possible be laid so that the outer rail of each line shall be at a distance of two feet three inches from the nearest curb thereto; and as to the remainder of the tramway and crossing places, the same shall be so laid as the commissioners shall determine.

The gauge was specified as three feet, and the promoters were required to maintain the road surface within eighteen inches of the outside of the rails, and reinstate the road within six weeks of any abandonment. The promoters had the right to alter their lines, subject to approval by the commissioners and the governor, but repairs that involved opening up the roadway were subject to seven days' notice and not more than 100 yards in every 440 were to be opened at any one time.

The Act incorporated a complex list of penalties for delay in completing repairs, including a fine of £20 a day for interrupting gas or water mains. The governor (upon application by the road authority) could require the promoters to adopt improvements in the tramway, and the road authority (with Tynwald approval) could require portions of the tramway to be lifted and relaid at the promoter's expense where inconveniently placed. The Prospect Hill section was subject to the commissioners widening the road at this point, and an inspector appointed by the governor was to approve the line before opening. The line was to be built within one year of the Act's promulgation (11 January 1896) and the works were to be substantially commenced within three months.

The road authority could specify the speed limits, the distance between following cars, and the amount of traffic on the route, and the 1876 Bay Tramway Act's red front and green rear lights were perpetuated. Hinting at trailer operation, the Act stated that '...at all times a bell shall be attached to the front carriage on such tramway which, by its ringing, will give notice that the carriages are in motion'. The promoters could make and exhibit byelaws concerning time-tables, interference with the line, passenger behaviour, etc. A person guilty of contravening them could be detained, and if unknown as to name and place of residence could be taken before the High Bailiff or a JP. Penalties were mostly the classic £5 fine, but for non-payment of fare only forty shillings. Removal of offending passengers was permitted, and those who could not pay a subsequent fine might find themselves sojourning for up to three months in gaol.

Passengers, luggage and parcels were to be carried, and fares were fixed in the Act. Those on the Bay line were to remain at 2d in summer and 1d in winter, whilst those on the cable line encouraged 'assisting' downhill loads by offering differential fares: from the Jubilee Clock to Woodbourne Road via Buck's Road in summer was to cost 2d uphill and 1d down, but the winter fare would be 1d. each way. Through fares of 2d uphill and 1d down* were also offered from Jubilee Clock and Derby Castle to Woodbourne Road via Ballaquayle Road, by changing from horse to cable-car at Broadway, this fare also becoming 1d each way in winter. Children

---

*But 2d for Woodbourne Road to Jubilee Clock via Ballaquayle Road downhill in summer, exceptionally, doubtless to prevent overloading of the bay line's busiest section.

Two views taken during construction, c.May, 1896. The upper is in Victoria Street, just opposite the former Thomas Street Methodist Church, the lower on Prospect Hill (only recently widened by demolition so as to allow room for <u>two</u> tracks).

S. R. Keig Ltd.

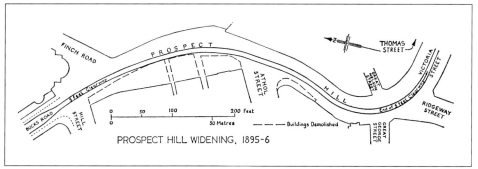

PROSPECT HILL WIDENING, 1895-6

A plan showing in detail the widening just mentioned   *J. C. Cooke*

under thirteen years of age were to travel at half fare, and the summer fares were to apply from Whit-Saturday to the end of September. Charges for luggage ranged from 3d to 9d for weights between 7lb and 56lb, and parcels exceeding 56lb in weight could be charged as the promoters might think fit, though they were not obliged to carry parcels exceeding 28lb.

As the roadway was marked out, Victoria Street tradesmen realised that cable cars would run only 2ft 3in from the kerb, and at once went to the improvement committee. Experimental tracks in Victoria Street from Duke Street to the Villiers hotel were used for a demonstration run by horse cars on 21 January 1896, including cars standing opposite each other while traffic passed between, watched by the improvement committee, the directors of the tramway company and the town surveyor, along with many traders. Later, at the commissioners' office, the traders urged that a double line be laid in the centre of the road instead of a single line along each side. After discussion with engineers Flett and More, Bruce agreed to do what was asked.

The *Isle of Man Times* warned Bruce that he was putting himself into the hands of his enemies by thus departing from the letter of the Act, and early in February this proved to be true; centrally placed track in Woodbourne Road, on a section specifically legalised for track at the side of the road, was found to be on top of the water main. By 15 February the entire work had stopped and between 200 and 300 men were laid off, the Press commenting that if the track were laid at the side it would be 'on the gas' and if in the centre, 'on the water'. Despite the formation of the new town council in March, only recourse to the Legislature could put things right and sort out the mess into which affairs had meanwhile drifted. An amending Act was finally signed on the morning of 13 May 1896, permitting the Victoria Street-Prospect Hill line to be laid as a centre-of-road double track with a four-foot clearway, increased to five feet on the Prospect Hill bend. Elsewhere, the line's original position was substantially maintained.

By 2 May cable track was being completed down from Woodbourne Road to Broadway, but only 1,000 yards had been laid by the end of the month; the rest was finished by August. The junction with the horse tramway at Broadway (mentioned in the Act) was apparently <u>not</u> built, although we

A later scene with Alexander Bruce (with beard) and other unidentified notables examining the full scale cable tramway point inserted in the northbound horse car track (the Victoria Street cable tracks had already reduced to a single line at this point). The terminal pit actually lay beyond the end of Walpole Avenue 'under' the horse tramway, in a section of roadway which (arguably) can be seen as part of the promenade, or of Victoria Street! Our text explores the mechanical consequences.

Dick, Kerr photo

have clear photographic evidence of cable trackwork being installed in the Bay tramway at the Victoria Clock.   There had also been protests over the intended operating speed of eight mph, and despite the company's protest the clerk of the Rolls insisted on six mph from Hill Street to Thomas Street and from Clifton Terrace to the foot of Broadway. Any such local speed limit on a cable tramway has a universal effect over the entire system.

On a site at the foot of the future York Road, the company built a power station and car shed, a pleasing structure in red brick. A corner of the land originally purchased was relinquished to form a public road, so as to give the tramway a better approach to Ballaquayle Road. They also bought two houses in Laureston Avenue which might be affected by the vibration, and let them to their workmen! On a sloping site, the buildings were on two levels. The upper part comprised a car shed 235ft long, 37ft wide and 15ft 9in high, with four tracks and access by a traverser. Each track held five cars, and each had a pit save at the far end, where, until the pits were extended in 1902, the grippers had to be detached to clear the solid floor. Next to this and 11ft lower was the boiler room, 62ft long, 27ft wide and 13ft 6in high, and beyond this was the engine house, 65ft long, 37ft 6in wide and 18ft 6in high, with a floor level 2ft 9in below that of the car shed. On the seaward side was an open yard, with bunkers for the coal.

The boiler house contained two hand-fired Galloway boilers, 30ft long and 7ft in diameter, working at 100lb/in². The boiler flues led to an 80-ft brick chimney. Auxiliaries included feed pumps and a Green's economiser that raised the feed water temperature from 60° to 250-300°F. The original water supply was by an underground tank below the firing floor, fed by a spring, but by 1902 this had been augmented by a 6,000-gallon elevated tank using town water at 2s per 1,000 gallons.

There were two high-pressure non-condensing engines of 250 hp, supplied by Dick, Kerr & Co, with 20in bore and 42in stroke, and with live-steam-jacketed cylinders externally cased in polished mahogany. Each engine was fitted with Dr Proel's governor and expansion gear, Corliss exhaust valves, and a 13ft 4in-diameter flywheel. Either engine could be connected by its flanged coupling to a centre shaft from which the winding pulley was driven by shrouded double helical gearing. The original drive included a Weston friction clutch, so that the engine might be loaded while running, but in later years direct drive was substituted and the engine had to be started against the dead load of the stationary cable.

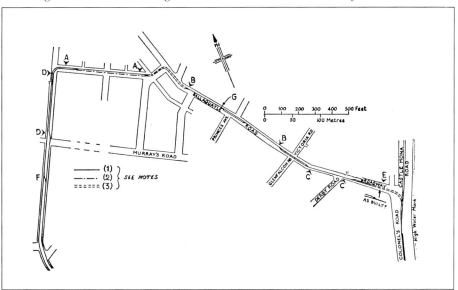

The most complex section of the Douglas cable tramway, from Woodbourne Road to Broadway, showing (1) track as laid in 1896, (2) track doubled in 1905, and (3) proposed tracks not built. For track layout between A-A and B-B as actually constructed, see ensuing depot plan. Tracks A-A and B-B were laid 4ft from the northern kerb, C-C 2ft 3in from the southern kerb, D-D 2ft 3 in from the western kerb with 5ft clearway. From Murray's Road to Hill Street the tracks were laid at opposite sides of the road. The line from G to E was closed in 1902 and cars then terminated at Stanley View (G); a crossover was added at F about 1927. The Avondale crossover (1896) lay just below the upper D, and was reused to construct F.

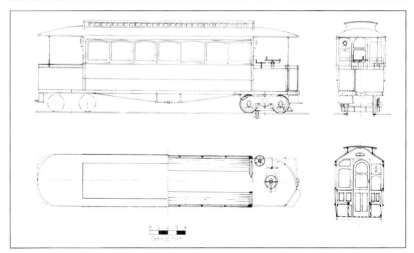

Closed cable car of 1896, series 79-82. The dotted lines show the car roof as built, the solid ones those on Milnes drawing in *Railway World*.   P Hammond

Here the cable was to start and finish its run. The incoming cable was passed round the grip pulley for nearly 75 per cent of its circumference, then round an adjacent idler to the ensuing idler pulley of the tension race. This, by its half-ton counterweight, kept the cable taut enough to ensure an adequate grip in the white-metal-lined groove of the driving pulley. Going out from here through a tunnel to the diverter pit, the cable next passed over pulleys arranged to turn it through 90 degrees and parallel to the surface of the road, and so continued eastward to Broadway, where the large pulleys of the terminal pit reversed its direction. Coming back along the opposite track, it passed over the cables leading to and from the power station and continued to 'Victoria Street's' terminal pit, (actually located beyond Walpole Avenue, opposite the flank of the Peveril Hotel), returning to the re-entry tunnel outside the depot. In this way, uphill cars had a continuous cable past the depot and only descending cars had to release and coast past the entrance.

Trackwork consisted of 76lb/yd Belgian rails laid on concrete, connected by tie-bars to cast-iron yokes laid 3ft 6in apart. Unlike American yokes, they did not have massive cast extensions to carry the running rails, a considerable economy in design. The concrete-walled centre conduit had upper edges formed by 38lb/yd slot rails bolted to the cast-iron yokes, and spaced to give a slot $^{11}/_{16}$in wide on straight track and $^{3}/_{4}$in wide on curves. The cable ran in this conduit, passing over an appropriate succession of 12-in diameter grease-lubricated pulleys. Pulleys used on straight track had bushes in lignum vitae, a naturally greasy wood. On straight track, the pulleys were vertical and generally 49ft apart, but on curves they lay horizontally and came as close as 3ft. The cable's direction of travel was reversed by two large pulleys in the terminal pit at Broadway and a similar pair at Victoria Street.

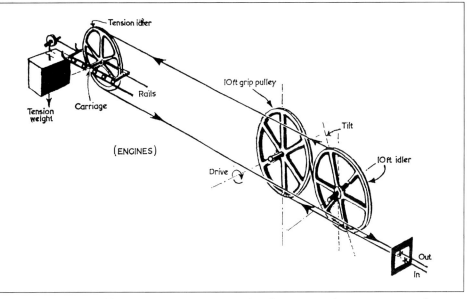

The internal cable circuit in the Douglas winding house. Note the ingenious use of a tilted idler.

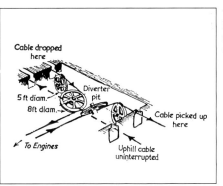

The diverter pit outside the winding house. Downhill cars dropped the cable and coasted across; the uphill cable was uninterrupted.

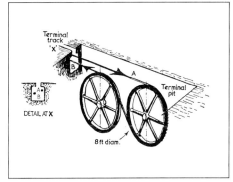

Terminal pit layout (Broadway and beyond Walpole Avenue).

A one-piece cable by Geo Craddock of Wakefield arrived early in July 1896. More than three miles long and weighing twenty tons, it came on two drums because of a fifteen-ton crane limit at Douglas. A later spare cable came from T. & W. Smith of Newcastle; both were hemp-cored, six-strand cables of $3^1/2$in circumference, each strand having thirteen wires. Two traction engines were used to haul the first cable up the hill to the engine house, but they slipped to a standstill and had to be helped by a windlass and ropes before reaching one of the two special storage drums in a rear extension of the boiler room.

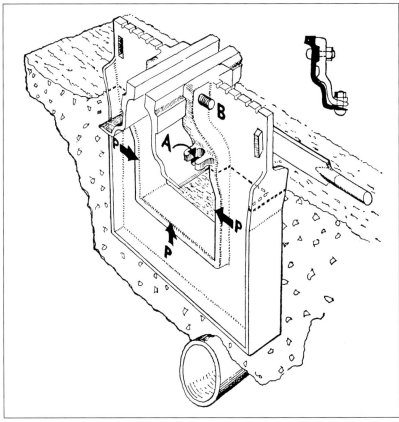

Douglas cable tramway: *(above)* a cast-iron yoke supporting the slot rails of the cable conduit, which were secured by bolts A and B; the profile of the concrete-walled conduit is shown by arrows P. The separate end view is of a twelve-bolt fishplate. *(Opposite top)* section through a pulley pit on straight track; arrow D shows the ...aximum depth of the car gripper, when fully engaged. *(Opposite Below)* a transverse section on curved track; this drawing also shows the twin-headed centre rail intended for use on Prospect Hill, before widening was agreed. A passing car displaced the cable as shown by the arrow (the inside of the curve is to the right as drawn).

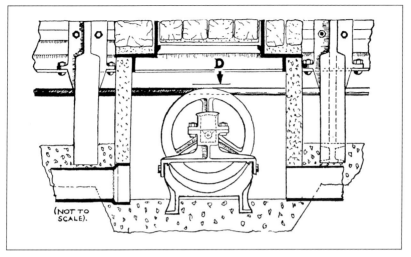

(NOT TO SCALE).

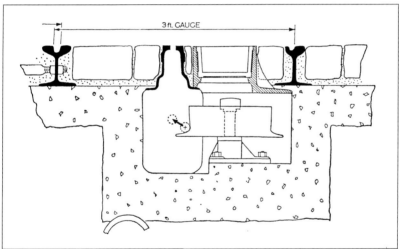

'Threading' began at 3am on Wednesday, 5 August 1896. The two traction engines picked up the cable end from the diverter pit and proceeded down to Broadway and back along the whole route as far as the Salisbury hotel, in Victoria Street, by 10am. Here a sewer excavation meant that a pilot cable had to be taken on to the terminal pit, opposite the flank of the Peveril hotel. By 1am on 6 August this was ready, and by 5am the main cable had been passed around the pulleys. The winding house was reached again after another $2^{1}/_{2}$ hours, and the exhausted men laid off for three hours. The eighty-foot splice needed to complete the circuit was begun at 11am the same day, and on Friday 7 August one of the engines was started to remove the slack, which was found to total

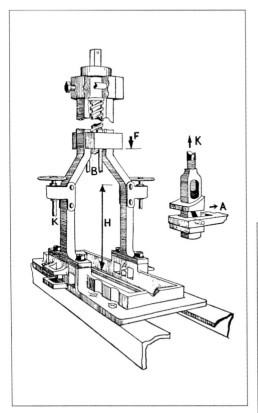

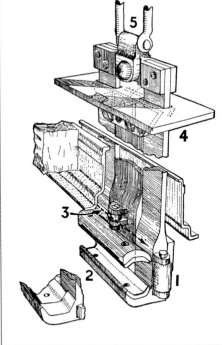

Upper and lower parts of Colam's gripper. The twin stanchions supported on the gripper foundation plate act as guides for the nut whose lowest position is shown by F. The handwheels K operate securing bolts A (see detail) which retain a loose plate to which the gripper's fixed jaw is attached. The nut when raised from position F normally closes the gripper jaws, but if the cable is removed and bolts A withdrawn the entire gripper unit may be drawn up through height H, lifting the gripper clear of the conduit through an access hatch. The rods B (numbered 5 on view of lower portion) allow the pull of the nut to be transmitted to the top frame of the moving jaw. 4 is the loose plate carrying the fixed jaw, 3 is one of the two side rollers (shown in relation to its bearing on the inside of the slot rails), and rollers 1 serve to align the cable with the centre of the gripper jaws (2), whose renewable soft metal jaws are also shown. The ratchet hand operates the gripper screw through its squared upper end. Baseplate '4' was later bolted in position rendering the mechanism worked by handwheels 'K' redundant. It is concluded that the open side the jaws faced the <u>near</u> side of the car at each end.

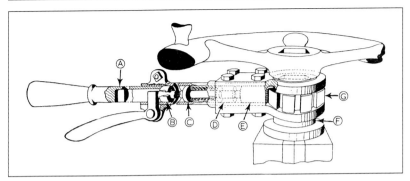

The gripper controls as used at Douglas, drawn from the surviving specimen. A copy was made for the preserved car c.1974, so it carries two. The gripper was applied and released by the hand wheel, and a ratchet handle served for the final tightening and initial release. Handle A could slide out for greater leverage. Sprung collar C kept the ratchet E dis-engaged during handwheel operation; to engage the handle, the trigger was lifted, moving the ratchet spindle through the collars B and D, engaging ratchet dog E with wheel G. F is a cylindrical collar on the gripper screw which spigots into the lower part of the handle assembly. Related credits: p.75, J. C. Cooke, p.77-82, Author.

thirty feet. A car was then sent out, and travelled down to the foot of Broadway and back.

Two grippers were used on each car, one for each direction of travel. As at Edinburgh, Streatham and Matlock, the grippers were of the type patented by William Newby Colam, who had been assistant to E.S. Eppelsheimer on the pioneer Highgate Hill line in 1884. At Douglas the grippers were single-sided, as junctions, etc, did not exist. The jaws of the Colam gripper were fitted with soft-iron inserts secured by white-metal rivets, and were thus readily renewed when worn. On straight track, the vice-like jaws of the gripper lifted the cable clear of the adjoining vertical pulleys, and on curves the gripper's side rollers bore against the inner slot rail and caused the cable to be pulled clear of each horizontal pulley as it passed, forming the apex of a triangle whose base was a line joining the pulleys on either side. Another important feature of the line was James More's slot brake, which consisted of vertical calliper jaws that gripped the slot rails from above and below when applied by a cross-handle.

On the afternoon of 8 August 1896, a car fitted with slot brakes was sent out to test the line but experienced difficulty on the Avondale curve. Next day James Walker, engineer to the Harbour Board, carried out the official inspection and reported on the 10th, specifying the length as about 1 mile 4 furlongs, 5.76 chains. The tramway consisted of a single line with four passing places for about 700 yards and the rest of the line was double. The most severe gradient was stated as 1 in 10.6.

Walker had carefully inspected the whole line, including travelling over it in a car and making some severe tests of both the ordinary and emergency brakes. He found that the latter required attention in order to

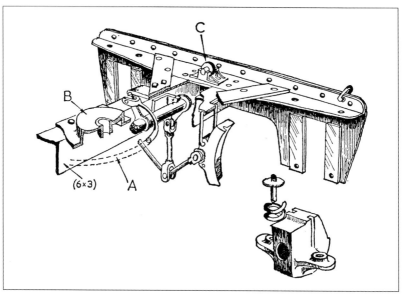

Bogie frame detail of Douglas cable car, with axlebox and spring detail shown separately. A is the link for the brake pull rod, B is the centre pivot, and C is the side bearing roller, later replaced by a block with a felt pad insert.

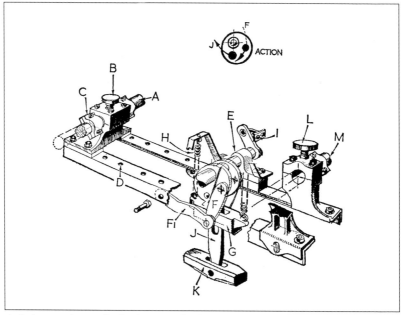

Axle-hung gripper plank, showing slot brake detail. A and M are the outer and inner axles, B and L are the suspension bearing greasers, C the locating collars which limit side travel to maximum slot displacement and D the holes to which the gripper assembly is bolted. The slot brake was applied by a pull on rod I turning discs on shaft E whose links F force upper shoe G down against sprigs H, while centre link J pulls shoe K against the underside of the slot rail. Links F1 absorb the resulting drag take the curve at Avondale House more easily and then wanted a trial made of the emergency brakes at Prospect Hill and Broadway. Finally, he wanted an 'alarum bell' fitted to each end of every car. He deputed his assistant, Mr. Nevill, to report to the governor's secretary, Mr. Storey, when these requirements had been met as the line would then be safe to operate.

Four days later, on Thursday, 13 August, Nevill was able to report that the inspector's requirements had been met. The warning bells had been obtained from Liverpool and were hung from the roof-edge timbering to the left of the driving position.

On Saturday, 15 August 1896, three cable cars entered service, providing a ten minutes frequency. The crews included three Manxmen, George Edward Lace, Edmund Butterfield and Robert Leary, who had spent the preceding six weeks training in Edinburgh, whilst men from London and Edinburgh had been brought to Douglas to train the others. Dr. Farrell also gave an exhibition of the art! George Lace, who died early in 1968, once told the writer that he believed that only four cars were on hand at the opening, and that the remaining eight (four open and four closed) arrived after the start of public service. (Photographic proof of this appears in our depot interior view).

The Press reported four cars in service on 17 August, and five by the following Saturday, 22 August; the full service (eight cars?) only awaited the training of further crews. The journey time was given as twelve minutes from the Jubilee Clock to Avondale, which would be fast even today.

These initial cars were numbered from 71 to 78, leaving 1-70 for the Bay tramway. They were roofed, 42 seat, cross-bench cars with bulkhead ends, having seven full-width benches for four, plus two other seats for four against the bulkheads and six (two doubles, two singles) on the platforms. Later (see illustration) one of the bulkhead seats was 'out of bounds' at the driving end. Alternate side pillars extended to the roof. From the restored car, the overall dimensions are: length 30ft, body width 5ft 7½in and height 9ft. The two bogies were of 3ft 6in wheelbase, and at centres. Sanding gear was fitted but later removed, the access traps survive in the end seats. The later arrivals, closed cars Nos 79 to 82, differed from the builder's drawing, suggesting that they were altered during construction. The overall length of these cars was 28ft 10½in, width 5ft 6in and height 9ft 10½in; other dimensions are apparent from the drawing. Interior lighting was by Colza oil lamps. The known platform seating (for 4) may have had a 'driving end' prohibition from the outset, lowering capacity to 30 (28 'inside').

On both open and closed cars, the complete route was displayed above the windows, the inscription reading 'VICTORIA PIER, VICTORIA STREET, BUCKS RD, WOODBOURNE ROAD, BALLAQUAYLE RD & BROADWAY'. On the open cars, a shaped, hinged flap, was soon added to obscure 'BROADWAY' when lowered, and thus cater for short workings to Ballaquayle Road. In later years lead gutters were fitted to these cars and the flaps removed. Notes on the livery of the cable cars appear at the end of the chapter.

To celebrate the year's innovations – the new promenades (completed

A group of excellent photographs appear datable to August of 1896, when George Lace recollected there being only four cars yet available. Consequently, that of the depot interior shows the far wall to be occupied by the gripper mechanisms of yet-to-be-delivered cars, whilst the boiler room view shows the boiler to the left as unused. The view of the engine room shows signs of use (there exists an earlier 'identical' view with no evidence of the gearing having been used, e.g. dull gear teeth). The exterior view of the building indicates its considerable extent and pleasant architectural style (a sketch is used to show the frontal aspect of the engine room).

Photographs by Warburton courtesy Manx National Heritage, sketch: Author

GEORGE F. MILNES & Co
BUILDERS
○ TRAMWAY & LIGHT RAILWAY ○
CARRIAGE WORKS
BIRKENHEAD, ENGLAND.

Milnes builders plate ($3^{11}/_{16}$in by $1^7/_8$in) one survives from preserved cable car 72/73'.   *J. C. Cooke*

(*continued from page 83*)
by June) and the cable tramway – a lavish two-hour procession was arranged for Wednesday 26 August. It was to start from the foot of Broadway, proceed round the cable tramway route and then along the entire series of promenades to Derby Castle terminus, returning to a public gathering on the new promenade fronting the Palace grounds, where there would be speeches from a dais by Lieutenant-Governor Henniker and others. The day was fine; horse- and cable-cars were all decorated for the occasion, as was the whole promenade, and ran where conflict with the procession could be avoided. The speeches were typical of their day, and the IOMT&EP Co and T.G. Taylor were specially commended. The three bands (Palace, Derby Castle and Foxdale) then resumed their afternoon performances, and in the evening Pain's W.E. Jolliffe provided fireworks from Derby Castle's pier and from the Tower of Refuge.

The following evening, 27 August, the tramway company and Dick, Kerr & Co provided a sumptuous dinner at the Douglas Bay hotel. The proceedings had begun at 3pm with a visit to the York Road premises, where George Flett and colleagues acted as guides. Dining notables included the Lord Bishop, Mr. W.B. Dick, and John Kerr; the guest list was widely drawn and included a full complement from both Dick, Kerr's and the IOMT&EP Co. Bruce was chairman, and claimed that as a result of the new service, property values in Upper Douglas had risen by 20 per cent. Dr. Farrell said that he could address himself to his toast ('The Contractors') for a fortnight, and wandered into philosophy, including the gem:

> Man wants but little here below
> As someone said before
> But when he gets it don't you know
> He wants a little more.

Over the first month, several stoppages occurred, none of which was serious. The curved sections of Prospect Hill required daily greasing of the horizontal pulleys, and the maintenance gang had to start at 6.30am. A soft cast-iron pulley at the Avondale corner was found to have a life of as little as seven hours, and a chilled iron replacement was soon put in. The Avondale curve had in the end to be eased, and while this was done a horse was used to haul short-working cars across the adjacent crossover, and at times around the corner itself.

What was the tramway really like? Imagine an early morning in the winter of 1896; in the relative darkness of the car shed, lit by a thin scattering of batswing burners, the shadowy forms of the cars sit over the deeper blackness of the pits. The duty car's oil headlight gleams yellow within its polished brass rim, with the obligatory red lantern panel lamp hovering above, whilst below the grippers hang down from their axle-borne supporting 'plank', (actually two parallel steel angles carried on each bogie), both ends having already been subjected to careful scrutiny

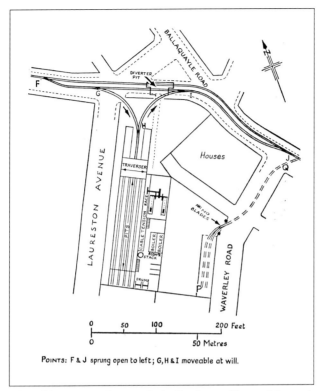

Points: F & J sprung open to left; G, H & I moveable at will.

The cable tramway depot and winding house. The track beyond
F was doubled after 1905 (the points F being removed) and the
track P-Q was laid after 1902 for access to horse-car storage.
The restoration of a car was undertaken at P.   *J.C. Cooke*

by the lamp of the shed fitter. Nearby, the steady pulsation of the engines
is partly masked by the more strident note of the main shaft gearing.

One of the duty men climbs aboard, and almost at once the harsh
metallic sound of a released handbrake is replaced by the faint hiss of
journals as the strong shoulders of his colleagues roll the car forward
towards the waiting traverser, to the accompaniment of an increasing
rumble from the wheel treads. Once halted on the traverser, the deeper
sound of the traverse is followed by a metalic click as the rails are locked
in line, and with a touch of the warning bell hung on his left, the driver
stands ready as the car is pushed out on to the descending curved track
leading east into Broadway. He applies his wheel brakes and the car
comes to a halt on the townward track, within earshot of a continuous
humming sound. After changing ends, this becomes a faint but insistent
vibration as a long slightly hooked flat steel bar is passed through the slot
and used to initially deflect, then allow the running cable to move
sideways into the lowered jaw of the leading grip, the headlamp,

meanwhile, being brought to the leading end of the car by the conductor.

With time for departure on hand, the driver takes up his stance, the slot brake screw column's handle, ahead on his left, the gripper to his right front, and the hand-wheel of the chain-operated wheel brake to the immediate left. Simultaneously he winds on his gripper and releases the wheel brakes, and the car moves forward, the rate of acceleration depending on the speed with which the gripper takes hold. A pull on the ratchet handle serves for the final tightening.

The ensuing ride is smooth and quiet, for although the hard paving and plate frame bogies would reflect any sound, the light cars in these early years leave the joints unhammered. Only a periodic flange squeal on the curves marks progress, with a concurrent rumble as the gripper's side rollers bear hard against the inner slot rail, and the occasional rhythmic traverse of pointwork.

Beneath the street, the passage of the tramway cable produces odd sounds from individual pulleys, which in some cases tend to ring with low, bell-like notes, and in summer cause visiting dogs from the mainland to stand in the road looking down the slot and barking at the noise. It also tempts local children to drop lengths of paper and string down the slot, to be caught by the moving cable and swept visibly along the road.

At a stop, the grip is released by spinning the gripper wheel and the wheel brakes are applied. (Strap operated bells were used for signalling in the normal way). The fierce-acting slot brake is only used in emergency or on the steepest grades, where normal service stops are avoided; even with sanding gear, wheelslip would be almost inevitable. On downhill sections, gravity gives the car a start, but in professional gripper operation the cable has always to pull the car, and never vice versa, a forbidden practice known as 'slipping the cable'. Approaching the terminal pits, the gripper-off, brakes-on sequence is repeated, and here the pulleys are arranged so that the cable runs to one side and leaves the opening jaws of the grip as the car rolls to a halt, whilst the returning cable comes within reach of insertion. The flat bar mentioned earlier could be used to push out a reluctant cable, if need be.

The odd layout at the Victoria Street terminus makes necessary an amplification of the preceding description of driving technique, in the process revising the comments in Isle of Man Tramways (1970) on the method by which a car was connected to the moving cable. Firstly, it has to be understood that alignment of the cable was necessarily to one side of the slot through which depended the gripper jaws, so that when a gripper jaw travelled along the slot it did not tend to displace the cable from its normal alignment (this does not apply to curves). Secondly, when a car stood on straight track with both its grippers raised, the engagement process saw (i) the moving cable deflected sideways ('away') with the flat bar already mentioned (ii) the cable allowed to spring back above the meanwhile lowered bottom jaw. When this was raised the car would begin to move. Reversing these steps 'in order', a car could be disconnected with equal facility, but the ability of a cable to be led off so as to itself leave the loosened jaw was a practice of the era. However, one could not continue past such a terminal installation.

Probably the earliest operational pictures published are the ones appearing in 'Railway World' for October, 1896. One of a car at the foot of Prospect Hill is impressive in its background (Dumbells Bank, no less) and also (when enlarged) gives a good close-up of car 72. Another (whose negative appears lost) now exists only in the magazine and is worth reproducing as representing the steeper part of the ascent.

Car 72: S. R. Keig Ltd.

A saloon car is depicted in Bucks Road, opposite Prospect Terrace, where the kerbside track is a prominent feature.   *National Tramway Museum*

Now, the situation at Walpole Avenue was highly non-standard, for the terminal pit was a 'remote' installation lying under nominally horse car tracks opposite the end of the one time Peveril Hotel. Did, therefore, the cables proceed at normal height through the terminal pointwork where 'double' became 'single' <u>and</u> thence continue through the cable points inserted in the northbound horse tramway track (so that a cable car might run on to the Bay tramway, finally to encounter a self-disengaging facility immediately before the terminal pit)? Or were the manual disengagement practices outlined in the previous paragraph employed, exclusively, at <u>both</u> the Douglas termini? We may never know. Descriptions by surviving eye witnesses cannot (obviously) <u>now</u> be re-examined with their co-operation. The deflection of the cable by crew is a case in point, where witnesses (mistakenly) assumed the cable was pushed into the grip jaws rather than allowed to find its way there via its own tension. Hopefully, the reader will have realised that semi-automatic disengagement at Walpole Avenue would render the option of continuing beyond to the horse tramway junction a mechanical impossibility! The non-mechanically minded may also need to have it explained that the effort needed to deflect even a steel cable tramway 'rope' sideways is quite small (consider the ease with which string on a tightly tied parcel can be pulled away from the parcel's surface).

So much for the driving technique; what of the route? The line as built comprised 1.38 miles of double track, and 0.184 of single track. Victoria Street's terminal spur was linked to the horse-car line (originally by a full scale cable tramway point), thereafter the cars ran directly on either hand of the centre line of the street, with a 4ft clearway, as far as the curve at Ridgeway Street leading to the foot of Prospect Hill. There, the 40ft radius curve required a wider clearway of five feet, and the track climbed the sinuous curves of the hill with this wider spacing until the junction of Finch Road where, at Government Office, the tracks diverged to the kerbside position originally intended for the whole line, each track being 2ft 3in from the kerb. An earlier plan showed this divergence planned instead at Demesne Road. Thus far, and onward to Avondale, the architectural surroundings on either hand remained little changed until the 1970s 'building boom' (a consequence of the arrival of 'offshore finance') transformed the Prospect Hill scene.

Just beyond Murray's Road, the seaward track swung across to join the other before negotiating the acute Avondale corner, again with a 5-ft clearway. A crossover joined the two tracks, and the ensuing sharp curves brought the tracks into what was later to be called York Road, the outer one being four feet from the northern kerb. The track now became single, and continued to the promenade as a succession of loops and single track, with two curves leading into the depot. In 1896, the vacant sites on each side outnumbered those built upon, but on reaching Ballaquayle Road the older properties on either side again survive little altered. Only below Glen Falcon Road, where the walled gardens of Villa Marina and smaller properties occupied the southern side of the still narrow 'Broadway', did the architectural scene differ greatly from today's. The double junction shown at the promenade is unconfirmed, and the section intended as interlaced track between Glen Falcon and Derby Roads was instead built as shown on our plan.

The line carried no less than 193,645 passengers from its August 15 opening to the end of December, against 91,776 for the previous bus operation. Dick, Kerr's Mr Windsor stayed on until January 1897. At the company meeting held on 8 March, 1897, Bruce described the cable line as a 'one time much maligned, but now highly appreciated, convenience ...' More than the statutory minimum service was still provided. The line was the largest single item in the £133,954 17s 10d spent during 1896 on new works and equipment, but this also covered the doubling of the horse tramway track on the Central and Harris promenades.

During 1897, the cable line experienced a stoppage on Whit Monday and twice in August, with ensuing chaos while workmen searched for the cause. As a result the year's passengers only reached 489,682: staff had spent days and nights in rectifying the faults. Bruce later hinted that the failures originated in drivers' errors, which had since been reduced thanks to one W. Moar, who had been recruited from Edinburgh. The cable line's working costs had become painfully apparent, with costs of 13.64d/mile against earnings of 8.93d; mileage run had been 72,995.

In 1899, 91,682 car miles were run and 633,624 passengers carried; the one-day maximum was 7,979, the cost per mile 14.45d, and earnings per mile 9.4d. The average earning per journey was only 1s 4d. To reduce power costs, in the spring of 1899 IoM&EP announced a plan to draw hydro-electric power from the Sulby River and install electric winding gear, shutting down the steam plant except in mid-summer.

On Saturday 3 February 1900, Dumbell's Bank collapsed, and with it the Isle of Man Tramways & Electric Power Company; Alexander Bruce

Another early scene at Avondale, opposite the newly built Newsome Terrace, with open country beyond. The hut relates to (probably contemporaneous) short workings in August 1896 when cars were able to use the crossover and thus avoid the problems then being experienced with the acute Avondale corner.   *S. R. Keig Ltd.*

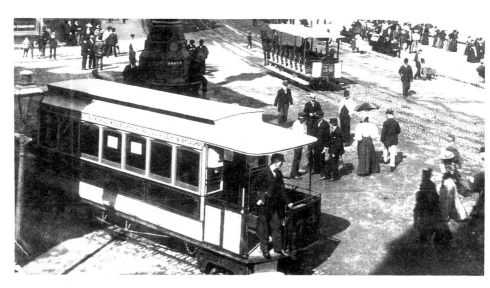

Half in shadow, saloon car 79 stands at the Victoria Street terminus, almost opposite the end of Walpole Avenue (whence comes the sunlight). The date is early c.1897-98.   Courtesy *Manx National Heritage*

had been the bank's general manager. The events that followed are described in '100 Years of the Manx Electric Railway' (1993). A delayed annual meeting held on 24 May 1900 was followed by others in an effort to keep the concern afloat, but liquidation came on 11 July and the whole enormous concern was put up for sale. W. H. Walker was appointed liquidator on 25 July, and invited offers for the purchase of the various lines.

Douglas Corporation saw their opportunity and on 22 October 1900 wrote to tramway valuation expert, Sir Frederick Bramwell, of Bramwell & Harris, asking for an assessment. They asked that he take into account 'the onerous conditions imposed upon the company for its concession' – truly an admission this, coming from the corporation! The cable line, they stated, was losing between £1,500 and £2,000 a year.

Bramwell offered the services of his partner, H. G. Harris, at a fee of 150 guineas and, this being accepted, Harris went to Douglas and completed his examination in one day. On 15 December he wrote to the company secretary for further information, and in July 1901 he submitted his report, a clear and concise summary of the lines, their physical state and their finances, quoting figures for both 1899 and 1900, since 1900 was under the cautious managerial policy of the liquidator. Those for 1900 were as follows:

Expenditure, Bay Tramway and Cable Tramway, 1900
pence per car mile

	Bay Tramway	Cable Tramway
Maintenance of way and works	0.75	0.58
Power and horsing	3.43	11.10*
Car repairs	0.27	1.55
Traffic expenses	2.07	3.99
General charges (office etc)	0.68	1.80
Sundries	2.84	1.25
Aggregated pence per car mile:	10.87	20.27

Totals for the year 1900:   £8,813 8s 1d   £6,184 17s 5d

*–4.35d on the cable and its repair, excluding steam plant.

He recommended a price of £50,000, and thought that conversion of both routes to electric traction would cost £105,000. In a later letter, he allowed that 'the cable tramways are a dead loss' and thought that the corporation need not be in any hurry to purchase, but could await the course of events. Nevertheless, by 12 August 1901 the corporation had tendered £40,000 and had been refused.

On 25 September their new offer of £50,000 was accepted. The Tramways Purchase Sub-Committee's report of 7 October explained at length the reason for the council's increased offer; the value of the two lines on the IOM&EP books had been £110,000, and any company buying them for £50,000 might well earn 5 per cent on its capital and also benefit

No 82 stands at the new Stanley View terminus, c.1902-03. The platform seating to which hinges were (to be?) added by the Corporation is visible behind the dash – this would have lowered known seating capacity to 30 (but there may well have been a driving end 'prohibition' before the hinges were added).

R. Hargreaves collection

from the enhanced value at the end of their concession. Up to £1,300 a year might be saved under corporation management. The last paragraph began: 'all municipalities aim at possessing the tramways within their boundaries . . .'

The corporation then applied to Tynwald for a loan of £52,000, repayable over thirty-five years. A special committee comprising Messrs Ring, Moore, Goldsmith, Kerruish, Kitto and Clucas, and presided over by Deemster Kneen, heard evidence on 13 November and 4 December 1901. H. G. Harris came to Douglas again, and emerged as a MICE, MIEE, council member of the Institution of Mechanical Engineers and vice-president of the Society of Arts. His valuations were based on the naturally poor year of 1900, and he contrasted superior 1899 results from an earlier company report. The £50,000 did not include the horse stud; the horsecar track was worth about £14,000, and the land and buildings amounted to £15,559.

Cruikshank, counsel for the corporation, summarised the passenger receipts for the cable and horse lines as respectively £1,586 and £11,191 in 1896, £2,717 and £11,953 in 1897, £3,041 and £12,232 in 1898, £3,577 and £12,861 in 1899, and £3,271 and £11,015 in 1900, ignoring cartage earnings and sales of manure. No cars had been run down to Broadway from York Road car shed since the beginning of 1901, though the cable still ran there in its conduit; the pit at Broadway had suffered from silting up. A replacement cable then cost £600 and was expected to last for fifteen months, though annual replacement had been allowed for. Contractor Mark Carine appeared as valuer of the real estate, and the next witness was Frederick Saunderson, who gave his opinion of the present day value as £65,125, and quoted current values for the materials, the cost of construction, rails, yokes, etc., which latter alone had totalled over 850 tons. Finally, Harris reappeared to give details of relaying of horse-car track carried out since the spring of 1900 and the town clerk showed that the town was well able to afford the intended purchase. The committee's report was favourable, and the purchase went ahead.

To close the main part of this chapter there follows an account of changes to the plant and working of the cable line carried out under corporation auspices. The purchase sub-committee had already obtained a report from Joshua Shaw of the IOMT&EP on the possible physical curtailment of the Broadway cable line, and on 20 December 1901 recommended that Shaw's scheme for a new terminus at Stanley View be accepted. On 24 December Shaw joined the new undertaking and took charge of the cable line at a salary of £10 monthly. He carried out the change between 21 and 28 February 1902, shortly before leaving the island to become electrical engineer to the Mersey Railway Company; his successor as cable-line supervisor was Arthur Tyson. On 25 March Shaw reported that the shortening of the cable had brought a fall in coal consumption of 8cwt in a fourteen-hour day, the previous daily figure being 3 tons 15cwt. The Depot – Broadway section had been described in 1898 by an IMR officer as 'almost unworkable', owing to the gradients and the narrowness of the streets; it is said that only two specified drivers had been allowed to take cars down to Broadway from the shed. The governor questioned the legality of the curtailment.

By 14 May track between Victoria Road and Derby Road was being lifted and re-used in extending the horse tramway on to the Victoria Pier. The rest of the abandoned track as far as Stanley View was removed later, and a low-roofed, two-road, horse-car shed was built in the yard adjoining Waverley Road. The access track abutted at about 75 degrees on to the cable track just above Stanley View, and the cars reached it by halting just opposite and being lifted bodily round, stern first, on to the access track. The corporation subsequently erected substantial stop signs around the route; having obtained management sanction the sole survivor was excavated from its Avondale shelter site by the author, who next secured an official 'stop' sign in its place, then wheelbarrowed the cast iron relic down to York Road – it later being set up in Derby Castle depot.

As implied, they also built a stone shelter at the Avondale corner. Horse-car overhauls, previously carried out at Derby Castle, were now done at York Road, the car being shunted over the connecting line at Victoria Street and towed from there by a cable car.

The four closed cars were insufficient for the winter traffic, and on 10 November 1902 the council agreed that open car No 78 should be

Another mid-1900s view of the Stanley View terminus shows its kerbside location. There appears to be a 'time clock' (or similar device) on the stop sign.   *J. H. Price*

enclosed. Its trial run took place on 14 January, and Mr J. Fargher received a (part?) payment of £20 for the work. The result was rather fine, Mr Fargher's elegant panelling being well set off by the varnished finish; the 28-seat saloon was 13ft 6in long, and the usual platform seats were retained. This de-luxe conversion may have proved a little expensive, for the next conversion was done on simpler lines.

On 9 December 1903, a sub-committee accepted a quotation from Messrs Faragher & Quiggin of £31 13s 0d to enclose cable car No 77. The result is shown in the photograph. The intended seating capacity remained the same. During November the corporation had been in touch with Dick, Kerr & Co. about speeding up the cable from its sedate six mph and providing a condenser for the engines, but nothing was done. In September 1904 spare parts were unsuccessfully sought from the LCC Streatham Hill cable line.

In 1905, the open cable cars were modified to allow easier carriage of luggage, by hingeing the bulkhead seats on the platforms, a notice forbidding their use (at the driver's end) being painted on their underside.* The saloon cars had similar end seat provision added in later years. Electrification of the line on the conduit system was considered in 1905, but rejected, and attempts to extend the cable cars to the Victoria Pier were rejected by the Harbour Commissioners. In June 1905 in an effort to combat competition and secure steamer passengers for the cable line, new additional tracks were laid to allow connecting horse cars to run from the steamers to the cable terminus in Victoria Street, as shown in the illustration.

---

*The preserved car still displays an original 42 seat capacity!

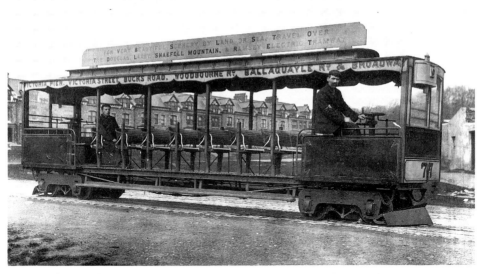

(Above) Cable car No 77 in York Road just before its rebuilding to saloon form in 1903. The roof gutters, lifeguard, and absence of sanding gear are the only changes from original condition. Driver John Thompson in command; (below) staff in the cable winding house at York Road, about 1908, Manager Stephen Robinson in bowler hat, senior gripman George Lace to his right, with child. Engineer Arthur Tyson in centre, with dog. *Both Douglas Tramway*

No 78 in York Road after its 1903 rebuild. The site to the rear was still not fully
built up. The roof advertisement is still an IoMT&EP one.   *Douglas Tramway*

On 13 December 1905, the corporation decided to double the cable
track between Avondale corner and the depot, and this was carried out in
1906. As a result, cars could no longer run downhill direct into the
depot; instead, cars arriving at Palatine Road (just above the depot)
dropped the cable there and continued by gravity down to Stanley View.
To enter the shed, they picked up the uphill cable to reach their run-in
position above the depot and then, with the cable dropped, coasted round
the curve and (with a skilled driver) just rolled on to the traverser.
Leaving the shed, a water can was always kept handy to wet the downhill
curve, making the task of pushing the cars out easier. The 'wye' system of
depot working ensured that the cars changed ends each day and evened
the wear. When next repainted, the wording on the car letter-boards
ended in 'WOODBOURNE RD, BALLAQUAYLE, STANLEY VIEW,
BROADWAY.'
     In February 1907, the corporation ordered two more 38-seat cable cars
from the United Electric Car Company of Preston; these arrived in June,
and cost £348 each. They took the numbers 69 and 70. Their design
owed much to Nos 71-78, but they shared with the new horse cars (Nos 43
and 44) the useful adjunct of sprung proofed canvas roller blinds, and had
full height pillars throughout. In February 1908, side screens for winter
use were fitted to the platforms of converted cable cars Nos 77 and 78.
     The year 1908 was marred by two fatalities, one of which occurred at
the top of Victoria Street on 21 April. The victim was a man of poor
mobility and eyesight – the cars could stop 'in two or three yards' – but
the corporation thereafter provided a safety flagman at this curve in

In an earlier publication a sketch of No 77 as converted was employed. A better image of the originating half tone illustration has now been located, here reproduced. *J. H. Price*

winter as well as in summer. The other (very rare) case was the death from heat stroke of cable tramway boilerman, William Kelly, on 3 July.

Another new cable car, No 68, came from G. C. Milnes, Voss & Co. of Birkenhead in May 1909. It has the usual seven cross benches and platform seating and resembled Nos 69 and 70 in being fitted with canvas blinds. Two-window end bulkheads were retained, with a lamp-box at the (rear) near side and a clerestory roof. In March 1911, Milnes Voss supplied another similar car, No 67, which had wooden roller shutters instead of the blinds. No 67 cost £325, and brought the fleet to sixteen cable cars. In the same year (1911) Sunday cable-car service was at last begun; Sunday operation had been an election issue in November 1906, and defeat had rewarded its proponents. The boilers' economiser was replaced during 1913. The tramway committee's accounts for the ten months to 31 January 1914 showed the usual disparity between the two corporation lines: the cable cars had cost £5,633 and earned only £5,163, whereas the horse cars had earned £21,547 against outgoings of only £10,327. Estimated cable-car earnings for the next two months were only £279 11s 10d, against expenditure of £969 16s 1d.

The cable cars continued to run throughout the 1914-18 war, with a reduced service, but their mechanical condition deteriorated. Evening cars would stop on the way down at Duke Street, where the driver would remove the splendid oil headlight and replace it at the rear, thus avoiding the danger of providing free illumination for German submarines!

By 1919, wear and tear on the cable line was causing concern and

The special trackwork installed in 1905 to allow a proper connecting service from the steamers to the cable cars, using horse trams. Exasperatingly, the cable conduit's slot and the 1896 conduit point are visually uncertain elements. A 'route' board from one of the 'connecting trams' survives on top of the 'cable car' display case erected by the Douglas Cable Car Group at the horse car depot.

Courtesy Manx National Heritage

A 'shipping view' of No 69 (or No 70) being placed on board the steamer 'Thursoy' at Preston Dock in June 1907.

United Electric Car Company photograph

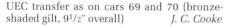

UEC transfer as on cars 69 and 70 (bronze-shaded gilt, 9¹/₂" overall)　　*J. C. Cooke*

Milnes Voss transfer as on cars 67 and 68.　　*Author*

arrangements for its short-term repair were put in hand. The estimates for 1921-22 provided £945 18s 2d for temporary cable track repairs and £1,260 for a new cable (against £649 in 1913). If the track was to be properly relaid this was estimated to cost £33,500. In the year to March 1920, the cable cars cost £9,740 and earned £7,156, the winter losses being even greater than before; during February and March 1920, the cable line cost the corporation £2,252 to run and earned only £645!

Until 1920, the cable cars had bulkhead oil lamps as on the horse cars, though acetylene lighting had been tried in 1908. The year 1920 saw a general change to acetylene lighting, the large and obstructive bulkhead oil-lamp box being replaced by a long and narrow acetylene-lamp box hung externally on the narrow panel above the heightened end window, with a hinged metal flap inside the bulkhead for access; thus considerably altering the end aspect of the open cars.

In 1920, the corporation bought five 26-seat Tilling-Stevens petrol-electric buses, and for the winter of 1921-22, these took over the cable route; thus shelving the renewal problem (the survivor was driven down to the harbour by the late Duggie Craine in 195(5): it now exists as a chassis exhibit). An earlier closure, from 9 April 1921, was probably due to the mainland coal strike; cars ran again from 24 June to 19 October, but thereafter complete winter closure occurred, and the season of cable-car operation grew shorter each year – for 1922, 16 May to 30 September, for 1923, 16 May to 17 September, and for 1924, 3 June to 17 September. For 1925, the period was 26 May to 16 September, and for 1926, 20 July to 28 August only. Meanwhile, the bus fleet grew apace.

To this point, nothing has been said of the working conditions experienced by the cable tramwaymen. The ensuing text would suffer materially if its references to the horse tramway men were deleted, and also contains some financial data concerning Corporation operations which again are part of an integrated account. By using smaller type this section of text will (hopefully) be more easily recognised as an 'interjection', relating to a wider sphere. The prominence of Stephen Robinson (DCT Manager 1902 to 1932) will be self-apparent.

'. . .In 1902 the profit to the end of March was £2,650, including retrospective adjustment. Stephen Robinson had now been appointed manager, and reported on wages and hours of work in Douglas and other towns. He proposed a winter week of sixty hours, instead of seventy. The rota would include long days of 12hr 40min, short days of 9hrs 25min, and relief days of 6hr 25min. Cable drivers now received

Part of a 2-car drawing by Peter Hammond, originally prepared to evidence the styling of Nos 67 and 68, at the time without direct photographic representation. It is now finally modified to show both cars in 'combination'. (It was only the blinds and shutters provision that distinguished the two cars). Both lost their lampboxes when given acetylene lighting, as evidenced by the view of 67 which follows. The vertical <u>grab</u> <u>rails</u> were also to be fitted to Nos 69 and 70, by the 'twenties.

A 'twenties view of No 77 passing 'Holmfield', on Woodbourne Road (today in use as Government offices). The nearer track, here in a kerbside location, seems to have been temporarily covered by recent gravel spreading. The driver (contrary to reported driving practice) has his hand on the slot brake handle: possibly the car had poor wheel brakes at the time?
National Tramway Museum

Another mid-twenties view shows an 'acetylene lit' car in a busy Victoria Street setting.
The late Arthur Tranter

24s a week, horse-car drivers 20s, and conductors 18s. In the year ended March 1904, £500 was paid towards the relief of rates, and by 31 March 1905 the total had reached £2,350. During 1905, Robinson prepared a report on motor buses, comparing the different makes available.

The cable line's winter deficit was such as to absorb much of the profit on the horse cars. Electrification might turn the loss into a profit, and 1906-8 saw several proposals for electric trams in Douglas. In January 1906, the Manx Electric Railway Co offered to lease and electrify the Bay tramway in return for royalty payments equal to the average net profit for the preceding three years, the aim (as in Bruce's time) being through-running from Ramsey and Laxey to the Victoria Pier. This the corporation unanimously rejected and instead they instructed Stephen Robinson to report on the electrification of both the horse and cable lines. There was also discussion of a new corporation electric line up to Peel Road and Circular Road via the North Quay.

Mr Robinson reported on 10 October 1906. The two tramways could be electrified for £77,820, the net expenditure after selling surplus property being £67,889. York Road would become the tramway power station, retaining the existing boilers and adding new generating equipment (£15,750). New track and foundations on the Bay tramway would cost £21,000, plus £2,100 for the overhead (with centre poles). New rails and filling in the conduit on the cable line would cost £11,000, plus £2,200 for the overhead. Alterations to the winding house would cost £3,500, and a traction battery £4,000. Ten new, 44-seat, single-deck bogie cars would be required at £710 each, and ten, 30-seat, four-wheel cars at £650 each. In addition, electrical equipment would be fitted to the (then) twelve cable cars (£4,620) and some of the horse cars would be kept as trailers.

Meanwhile, the tramway superintendent was already pressing for ten more covered horse cars, five 'toastracks', and three cable cars, but only two horse and two cable cars were ordered in February 1907. In July, the corporation obtained powers to run buses, and after an offer from Joshua Shaw of Mersey Railway motor buses was considered and declined, a contractor was engaged to run what proved to be a markedly unprofitable wagonette service along Peel Road. The conductors, who still had neither uniforms nor overcoats, agitated for a fifty-six hour week in place of sixty.

Also in 1907 the corporation set up a special committee to report on municipal electricity supply, which would have involved a new generating station capable also of supplying the tramways. The combined undertaking was estimated to cost not less than £100,000, which put it out of court. Manx Electric Railway now repeated their 1906 offer, but after some months of discussions they were finally and firmly rebuffed (in August 1908). This was the last serious attempt to provide Douglas with electric tramways, and most of the town retained gas lighting until the 1920s.

The maximum turn of duty for a tram horse in 1909-11 was eight journeys, but there was no similar limitation for the men. All horse-car men in 1911 received 28s 6d a week for unlimited hours, and in summer the working week sometimes amounted to as much as 114 hours. Cable drivers now earned 32s a week and conductors 24s 6d, but when Sunday cable cars were instituted in 1911 the crews were at first expected to work them without extra pay. The committee then offered a 73-hour seven-day week instead of the previous 78-hour six-day week, but the men wanted a six-day week of 72 hours, with Sunday paid separately, or another day off in lieu. The horse-car men were now demanding 32s 6d for a specific week of 84 hours.

A strike was planned for 13 July 1911, but on Monday, 10 July, an altercation between Stephen Robinson and three cable men ended in what the manager stated to be their voluntary departure, but what the men claimed was their dismissal. Both tramway sections promptly ceased work. The cable men returned to work the same evening, having secured a settlement giving them 30s and 27s for a six-day week of 72 hours, with separate Sunday pay. The horse-car men stayed out until 11.30 on Tuesday, and gained a 72-hour six-day week at 27s, with overtime payment and an extra 4s 6d for Sundays. No overtime was worked on the cable line. To recoup their outlay, the corporation could now charge higher fares, an amending Act to that of 1895 having been obtained on 14 May to allow fares of 2d downhill during the summer from Stanley View.

In the year ended 31 March 1914, the tramways paid £1,700 to the relief of rates. The horse cars had made their usual profit, earning £21,547 in the first nine months against costs of £10,327, and the cable line had earned £5,163 against costs of £5,633. A bus service newly instituted along the Peel Road with the first corporation motor buses had cost the department £177 and only earned £82, and the fleet stood at forty-five horse cars, sixteen cable cars and three buses.

With the outbreak of the 1914-18 war Douglas became something of a ghost town, with Cunningham's camp and other suitable areas converted to floodlit internment camps. The holiday industry rapidly became a mere shadow of its normal self, and transport services operated 'winter' schedules all year.

Labour relations in the island changed. Until 1917, the Isle of Man had no effective non-craft unions, but Alfred J. Teare and his associates realised that advancement for working people could best be obtained by forming a Workers Union; its first secretary was Charles Duncan, MP for Barrow-in-Furness. This catered for all the semi-skilled, such as transport platform staffs, and about fifty men attended the inaugural meeting on St Patrick's Day of 1917. Social legislation was almost non-existent in the island, for in the absence of taxation such things as old age pensions were not regarded as feasible.

In July of 1918, the wartime flour subsidy was withdrawn in the island, and the 9d loaf became 1s. A 'bread strike' took place on 4 and 5 July on this issue, and the horse, cable and electric cars (and outgoing steamers) stopped until midday on 5 July when, amidst rejoicing, the 9d loaf was restored. Underlying this was continued pressure for an island-controlled income or similar tax that would make possible the introduction of old age pensions and similar social benefits, first sought by Teare and his colleagues in 1909-10.

In the first postwar season, 1919, 343,332 visitors came to the island, against 615,726 in 1913; the Steam Packet Company's fleet was at only half its 1914 capacity. Costs had risen considerably, and for the year to March 1920 the cable cars cost £9,740 against earnings of £7,156, whilst the horse cars had cost £17,453 and earned £29,804. By 1921 the horse and uphill cable car fares had risen to 3d, with 2d downhill. A cargo of coal now cost 54s 6d/ton.

During 1920, with visitors totalling 554,350, the department's total expenditure, including sinking fund, reached £50,422 against earnings of £62,067. The renewals fund at £7,273 was faced in 1921 with relaying the Queen's Promenade section and the ex-cable rails on the Victoria pier, at an estimated cost of £6,768. Maintenance of the (by now) sixteen cable cars had cost £724, against £826 for the forty-four horse cars. Mr Robinson was granted a rise, none the less . . .

There were secret daredevils among the cable line crews. Early one morning two policemen sheltering in the porch of St Mary's Church (opposite Finch Road) saw a car hurtle down Prospect Hill, the driver slipping his cable. After a moment's thought, they followed it to investigate the anticipated 'pile-up' – and met it at Duke Street, intact, on its way back! Wear and tear had by now made operation so noisy that the seasonal Sunday service was always withdrawn during the hours of church service. During these intervals two cars normally stood opposite the former Grand Theatre in Victoria Street, ready to resume operations. Whence the noise? On straight track, the vertical pulleys had worn unevenly, producing as they revolved substantial thumps whose vibration reached adjoining properties. Corrugation by now affected the inside rail of many curves, and the closed cars (nicknamed 'Devils') suffered from window rattle and acted as an amplifying box. Chilled-iron disc wheels were not of the quietest, especially when associated with plate-frame bogies. The points had a fixed mate on the inside, and these had worn considerably. The worn cable varied in thickness, and at stops the gripper had to be left well loosened, but even so it vibrated and rattled as the cable slid over the lowered bottom jaw.

On the sections with kerbside track, other difficulties arose. At least one dray horse, habitually seen waiting outside premises on the Buck's Road section, had fully conditioned its thinking to cable tramway peculiarities. When an approaching car pulled up and sounded its gong, the horse would take itself and vehicle to the centre of the road, look round to check the clearance, wait for the car to pass, and then return to its roadside stance athwart the tracks!

The cable-car line was destined to survive for three more years as a seasonal transport ghost. Indeed, it became moderately profitable, typical earnings being £3,336 19s 2½d in 1928 against an expenditure of £2,468 9s 9d. In that year (from 24 July to 1 September) it ran 22,327¼ car miles and carried 216,639 passengers, against 35,538¼ miles and 336,970 passengers in the slightly longer season for 1927, from 1 July to 4 September.

In 1927, the Salisbury Terrace crossover was moved to Woodside, south of Murray's Road, where cars could coast through it down hill and so provide economical short workings. With the running lines on opposite sides of the road, the new installation looked decidedly odd. No special destination was now shown on these short workings, for the preceding car to Stanley View waited for that following and any through passengers were allowed to transfer. At about this time, road widening between Hilary and Derby Roads left the townward track remote from the kerb.

However, the end had to come, for the thirty-three-year-old trackwork and pulleys were worn out and the corporation bus fleet was now of adequate size. The 1929 season was the shortest yet, from 23 July to 19 August, with only 11,968 car miles and 78,981 passengers, the effect of the mainland's slump being apparent. The last day's traffic returns, for Monday, 19 August 1929, were receipts of £27 17s 4d, made up of 1,978 3d fares, 216 2d fares, 138 1½d fares and 115 1d fares, with 2,447 passengers carried on 192 car journeys and 528 car miles; there were also 219 journeys by contract holders. The end had come, and the *Isle of Man Times* wrote: 'What a strange quiet place Douglas was on Tuesday, the clanking noise had gone – the cable trams had stopped. Monday was their last day – perhaps for ever'. In their last season, the cable cars had cost £1,482 15s 10d, and had earned only £1,010 10s 3d.

The cable was soon drawn out of its slot, and the considerable task of filling the conduit and lifting the track was put in hand. The job took at least three years, Bucks Road being left until 1932. The last trams to use

The stone shelter erected at Avondale corner, with the cast iron stop sign column later preserved.   *Stan Basnett*

the line may have been horse cars hauled by motor vehicle on their way to York Road for winter storage and overhaul; thereafter these transfers were carried out by using a special low trailer consisting of two rails set to 3ft gauge and embodying some cable tramcars components. The depot was altered to serve as the corporation's omnibus depot, with the engine house and boiler room serving as the paint shop and joiners' shop, respectively, and the former open yard converted to become, partly, additional depot accommodation. Specimens of the tramway cables used in different years were preserved by the transport department, together with a gripper handle and car headlight, and one of the large tilted diverter pulleys and its access tunnel were still there beneath the roadway, though invisible to a passer-by; the turnel served as a rifle range!

The winding engines were broken up on site, and the sixteen cars were all sold to Charles McArten of Spring Valley. His intention was to convert them to holiday bungalows, and two of the original open cars of 1896 (Nos 72 and 73) survived until July 1968, heavily disguised but still on bogies, as the main part of a dwelling near Jurby. One car (and parts of the other) were then

A 1960s view of the cars at Crawyn, whilst still in residential use. Following purchase, the 'loose furnishings' acquired (and today of some value, but then discarded) included a chamber pot and a wooden-rollered cast iron mangle!

Stan Basnett

rescued for restoration and returned to the York Road premises which they had left almost forty years previously. The rest of the cars were broken up, as residential use did not eventuate.

Cable tramway fleet at maximum, 1911 to 1929

Fleet Numbers	Type	Builder	Date	Seats
67	Cross-bench car with wooden roller shutters	G.C. Milnes, Voss & Co.	1911	38
68	Cross-bench car with canvas roller blinds	G.C. Milnes, Voss & Co.	1909	38
69,70	Cross-bench car with canvas roller blinds	United Electric Car Co.	1907	38
71-76	Cross-bench cars without side blinds	G.F. Milnes & Co.	1896	38
77	Originally as 71-76, rebuilt 1904 as a combination car	G.F. Milnes & Co.	1896	38
78	Originally as 71-76, rebuilt 1903 as a combination car	G.F. Milnes & Co.	1896	38
79-82	Unvestibuled saloon cars with corner entrances	G.F. Milnes & Co.	1896	32(?)

Nos.79-82 seated twenty-eight passengers on longitudinal seats in the saloons and (theoretically) another four on double seats on the platforms. Photographs do not reveal whether other seats were placed to the left of the entrances to the saloon. There was certainly room for one (or even two) at each end. The open cars had seven benches seating four each, and were known to have had six small seats on the platforms. Nos. 72 and 73, when dismantled at Jurby in 1968, revealed original bulkhead seats for four at each end; these gave an original capacity of 42, revised to 38 from 1905.

The complexities of cable car livery only became really apparent when the restoration of '72/73' allowed investigation of paint 'relics'. As the owners of the 'bungalow' employed for protection tar of a particularly adhesive quality (in combination with multiple layers of roofing felt) the prospects did not appear bright, but eventually we had (i) a varnished ash body pillar with the chamfers picked out in red; (ii) an end body panel with traces of blue paint and (iii) most miraculously, much of the word 'Broadway' in its present colours. The latter survival was extraordinary – when the car destinations were amended to read '. . . Stanley View, Broadway' the spacings were made quite different and it happened that, whilst the rest of the car's 1896 lettering seems to have been totally removed, the last part of the route lettering consisted of two layers of paint and lettering, of which the 'residential' tar coating had only

The skeleton of 73 revealed in the foreground, the floor of 72 at the rear. This photograph was followed by the lowering of the roof of 73 on to the floor of 72, using the surviving body pillars as a 'hinge'. The team of around 5 or 6 (including some casual visitors) then discovered that the roof became '12 man heavy' as it approached its destination. The ensuing and uniformly achieved 'let go NOW' was executed with a precision born of extreme apprehension . . . ! (July, 1968).

J. C. Cooke

destroyed the outermost. The hours expended in carefully stripping the 'letterboard' looked as though they had been wasted until . . . ! The superb numerals and lettering executed by the late Ron Kitchen of Preston stemmed from this happy find.

The saloon cable cars of the group 79-82 present a difficulty, since our otherwise excellent Stanley View photograph does not reveal whether the car's side panel was of varnished teak, or was painted. The open cars used paint for their end upper panels, but traditionally Milnes saloon cars seem to have favoured varnish (but not universally). It is unlikely we will ever know.

The change to the destination sequence including 'Stanley View' applied from 'new', of course, to all the post 1901 cars, e.g., Nos 69 and 70 and Nos 67 and 68. The extensive appearance of the 'biscuit' livery by the 'twenties (see No 67 photo) raises questions as to whether this introduced any variation in the background coloration, the wording being presumably the popular straw yellow of the period.

Preservation Postscript

Before summarising the story of the surviving car's 'rescue,' transport and restoration it seems desirable to set the scene in a little more detail so far as the York Road depot is concerned. When the tramway closed the

An early phase in the body rebuild sees the roof on its new ash pillars.

Stan Basnett

main depot building was quite readily converted to garage use, and a substantial space was obtained by roofing over part of the yard parallel to the former engine room. A large smithy under the far end of the former car shed continued in use; dating from its tramway days the Author seems to recollect its still-displayed certification (allowing 40 men to be employed there!).

The Corporation 'bus fleet of pre-war and immediately post war years was a petrol engine dominated affair, and a machine shop annexe bridging the space between the old boiler room and the car shed at the bottom of the yard contained some pretty ancient machine tools (the larger number tramway inheritances, for the most part). When the Author sought to use the biggest of the lathes, c.1974, its location under a leaky roof made it reluctant to 'return to service', the drive belts preferring to slip rather than revolve the headstock spindle. Halcyon days . . .

More pertinently, the completely traditional Corporation garage image was still fully evident during 1950s' visits, when prior to his tragic death on Winter Hill 'Duggie' Craine, the Corporation's engineer, held sway. The place was spotless, with a depot cleaner who included polishing <u>all</u> the brass door furniture as part of his daily routine!

Disused by 1960, there were intriguing special 'shop' areas in the machine shop for such things as servicing magnetos, but the former engine room was a busy place until Corporation days came to an end, as here 'bus painting took place using totally traditional skills – the work done here by the Corporation team for the 1976 horse tramway centenary was exemplary.

As mentioned earlier, the boiler room itself saw use as a joiners shop – the (later) enclosed stores area at the far end still had some cable tramway 'bits' in its innermost recesses, for example lignum vitae bearing bushes formerly used for lightly loaded vertical cable pulleys (in the conduit). The cable tram restoration itself came to be executed at the innermost end of the long 'single decker' horse tram shed adjoining the seaward boundary wall, which at its extremity narrowed due to the presence of a tyre store.

The two areas of the depot least altered from cable tram days were the

As the countdown to the 1976 horse tramway centenary procession accelerated the Author had to turn his attention from bodywork to bogies (encouraged by his daughter). Most of the handling came to be shared with Stephen Broomfield (seen on the roof) – it was found that Milnes' cable tram bogies were 'two man handling' affairs, capable of assembly with that number of personnel without any lifting tackle. Manx helper Richard Davis is seen to the L.   *Manx Press Pictures*

Engineers Office and the ticket office. The former retained all its 'nineties furnishings, including a door glazed in the fashion of the time and containing the brass 'Engineers Office' letter box later retrieved for the Cable Car Group's display at Derby Castle. On the wall hung the case of cable specimens now also on display at the horse car shed. The ticket office still had its long counter and row of glazed screens and opening panels at which 'pay ins' took place (these rooms led off respectively right and left of the entrance). Until Mr Craine's death (27 February 1958) little change took place.

Later, in declining years, the storekeeper rose to become 'bus fleet engineer, then was replaced by a senior fitter – sadly the latter (with whom the Author developed a good working relationship) died following recurrent serious illness. Joiner Alec Corris, who bore the brunt of the incursion of cable tram 'amateurs', is still very much with us, continuing to work on the horse cars at Derby Castle.

Coming to 'how it was done,' the outline which follows (with minor changes) was originally published by the Group in its booklet 'Cable Tram Days'.

'. . . It was whilst writing Isle of Man Tramways (1970) that a Manx friend drew attention to the existence of two cable cars used as a dwelling at Crawyn, Ballaugh, near the Killane River. When it was learned that the owner, (the late Mr John Keig) had built a new home alongside, approaches were made on 'our' behalf by Mr W. Bagnall of Ramsey with a view to their purchase. By this date, the author's involvement in literary terms had fired an ambition to preserve something a little more three-dimensional and with three fellow enthusiasts the purchase money – a modest enough sum – was put together. This transaction was finalised on 7 January, 1968, and there began the not over-simple task of removal and restoration. Not being of 'independent means', the first step was to find some (!) and a succession of pictorial publications formed a happy solution to that problem – at least, initially. Latter day events saw expenditure gain a major lead over income . . .

The Cable Car Group's replica track section. The 'cast iron' yoke is actually a hollow fabrication, but the rails are genuine sections, sawn to suit. The setts are of Preston origin!   *Constructed by the Author, photo P. H. Abell*

In practical terms, we were granted an indoor work site in York Road bus garage, which though nearly devoid of daylight was dry and secure – one could return after twelve months and find things just as they had been left. When working 'across' (on the mainland) this security was a great incentive and encouragement. In the event, about one-third of the car came to be shipped from the Island to Preston, underwent restoration and then returned for assembly, with a labour force averaging about '2.75' persons over the entire period – happily, in 1976, Manx helpers came to the fore and allowed accelerated progress. The following represents an abbreviated 'restoration diary' . . .'

'. . . Summer 1968: Cars extricated from their 'bungalow' accretions and parts subsequently removed to York Road depot (25 July).

1969: Welded repairs to sides and ends of No 72's underframe, with attention to other details.

1970: Renewal of end planking of floor, following fitment of new curved channel ends to underframe.

1971: Roof (ex No 73) cleaned of multiple felt cladding and raised on eight new body pillars. Four side screens also fitted, using parts from 72 and 73. It was decided to give the car dual numbers, 72 and 73.

1972: Bulkhead framing installed.

1973: Bulkheads panelled and beaded.

1974: Seating made and trial fitted. Brake gear control elements re-installed.

1975: Bogies cleaned and repaired, minor body details continued.

1976: Car body painted, bogies completed. Car loaded and moved to Derby Castle depot, where finally assembled and ran in 9th August's horse tramway centenary procession* . . .'

By 1978 it had been possible to add a display case (designed and built by the Group) and, later, a track exhibit was constructed and shipped across to the Island. Below-road elements still have to be made up, possibly using timber vs. metal components, as the latter would be costly items. Meanwhile, over the period up to 1995 the car accumulated a respectable mileage using Land Rover propulsion (plus a gravity run technique developed for the descent from Summer Hill to the terminus!), but in the latter year became a battery electric, using the expertise of Mr Derek Shepherd, its operation by Isle of Man Railways being by special agreement with Douglas Corporation.

The Group continues to fund itself from donated income: Treasurer John B. Matthews, of 26, Sunningdale Drive, Onchan would welcome any such payments (to 'Douglas Cable Car Group') at that address. The closure and demolition of York Road depot is dealt with by Mr Basnett in Chapter 4.

Upper Douglas ticketing – 1996 notes by F. K. Pearson including data from Mr W. H. Bett

The ticketing history of the Upper Douglas tramway falls into two periods – that of its ownership by the Isle of Man Tramways and Electric Power Co. Ltd and that during Douglas Corporation ownership. Survivals from the former seem to consist of one solitary example, found by Mr Julian Edwards in the drop light of a Manx Northern carriage! This is one for either of two descents: Woodbourne Road to Broadway or Murray Road to Victoria Pier, the fare being 1d. The Cable Car group have a slightly later blind formerly fitted to the nearside windows of the open cars which advised passengers of the statutory '2d up, 1d down' differential, and which yet awaits a display case. By 1899 (the ticket shown is earlier, c.1896) the sections were more logically Avondale to Victoria Pier and Avondale to Broadway (the distance from Murray's Road to Woodbourne Road is about 140 yards, but it seems unlikely that a car would run from the crossover at Newsome Terrace to Murray's Road empty!).

The earlier Corporation era cable tram tickets in Mr Bett's collection were 1d green and 2d white, with the fare overprinted in red – these were styled to permit their use in either direction on both the promenade and Upper Douglas route(s), which now terminated at Stanley View. The later extensive development of Corporation ticket varieties preceded the cable tramway's closure, though its main impetus lay in widening motor 'bus operation.

In earlier text concerned with wages and conditions and Corporation operating finances will have been noted a reference to the May, 1911 Amending Act which permitted variation from the fares originally specified in the 1896 Act. The overall 'fares' story is one requiring further

---

*The true centenary date was 7th August – the 9th was chosen to avoid traffic congestion.

investigation (if in fact coherent evidence can be located). Typically, by 1928, 'all the way' cost 3d, and Mr Bett had a 2d short stage ticket in his possession, pink, with a lower half overprinted in purple allowing cable tram route travel from Victoria Pier to Rosemount or from Rosemount to Stanley View (this was therefore an 'uphill' fare with the reverse costing 1d?) and headed 'Douglas Corporation Trams and Buses' as now the latter ran Upper Douglas 'out of season'.

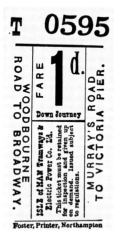

Two Upper Douglas tickets. T0595 dates from 1896/97 (reverse also shown) whilst the Corporation example is taken from a replica. *Julian Edwards and Author*

Menu cover from the celebratory dinner held at the Douglas Bay Hotel
Railway World & Douglas Tramway

Chapter Four

The Routes Today
— perambulations compiled by Stan Basnett

A WALK ALONG THE ROUTE OF THE CABLE TRAMWAY

How shall we follow the route of the Upper Douglas Cable Tramway when there is no longer any visible signs that it ever existed?

Well you will have read this book thus far so you will have a good idea of what made the tramway work and how it came to be. Now all we need to do is relate it to the ground and compare the present day Douglas with what it was like in 1896.

My own clear recollections go back just over fifty years, but that is not enough. I need some help in the form of the County series Ordnance Survey maps of 1869 and Browns Isle of Man Directory, together with family recollections and conversations with elderly people who just remember it in its later years.

We shall start the walk along the route of the former cable tramway at its Victoria Street terminus almost alongside the Jubilee Clock. In fact if you take a look at the inscriptions on the clock you will see a very close connection with one of the principal players in the scheme of things. Go across to it and read the inscriptions and if you have been paying attention to the book so far you will see what I mean.

Within the paved area in front of Busheys Pub you will see a short length of rail which was laid with a view to placing a replica of one of the cable trams at this location. This rail is not part of the original tramway, but it will do as a convenient starting point.

Look up Victoria Street and try to cast your mind back as I try to paint a word picture of what it was like. This grand street was driven through a number of narrow lanes cutting through Fort Street, Duke Street and Thomas Street in the process. Its purpose was to connect the new Loch Promenade and the low water landing pier which was named The Queen Victoria Pier on completion. The pier still remains although lengthened and widened.

The pier was completed in 1872 and Victoria Street completed in 1875 with Loch Promenade being completed about 1878. Where we are standing was all reclaimed land and twenty years later there would be a cable tramway providing much needed public transport to the newer part of the town. The rate of expansion and disruption must have been tremendous.

The wonderful building on the left was the prestigious and appropriately named Grand Hotel with the Grand Theatre and heated sea water baths. Later a Yates's Wine Lodge was to occupy the ground floor. On the right was the Villiers Hotel fronting the corner with Victoria Street and Loch Promenade and with entrances onto both streets and with an imposing array of shops at ground floor level. The building, now demolished, was still there when I last wrote a description of this route in 1990 in a book in the Rail Trail series entitled 'The Isle of Man by Tram Train and Foot'.

We are standing at the Victoria Street terminus. Below the ground was

114

the terminal pit which housed the two pulleys around which the cable ran changing the direction of the trams all as described in Keith's text. The tramway actually joined into a single 'terminal' track here from the double tracks that ran up Victoria Street. From this track a connection was laid (in 1896) to the Douglas Bay Horse Tramway, as explained in Keith's text. In 1905, added pointwork divided the track to connect to both the tracks of the horse tramway. The connection also allowed horse trams to be taken behind a cable tram to the depot in York Road both systems at that time having passed into Corporation ownership.

As soon as the descending tram entered the terminal track it dropped the cable and came to rest on its brakes. To commence its ascent to upper Douglas the driver would pick up the returning uphill direction of the cable with the gripper, release the brakes and head off on the left hand track up Victoria Street.

Off we go then up Victoria Street soon passing on the left what was the Salisbury Hotel. Look at the whole of the frontage and in particular above the entrance at the ornate filigree work in the tympanum. The horses and chariot in full flight are carrying the Greek sun god Helios driving the sun across the sky. Why you might ask? Well the answer is that when the cable cars were passing here the hotel was named The Sun Hotel. Its description in adverts of the day describe it as a first class commercial hotel and assures us that the proprietor, a Mr John Parkes, has taken great care to secure everything conducive to health and comfort. We are assured that the hotel speciality was 22 year old brown brandy and that a porter attends every steamer to convey passengers' luggage to the hotel free of charge.

From now on Victoria Street has changed greatly with newly built offices occupying much of the streetscape. The block of properties on the right before we reach Fort Street contained two dining establishments which were in a class of their own and they lasted until 1972. They didn't open until five years after the tramway started. Trading as Wilsons and Clagues Silver Grill their trademark was the sight of the chefs carving the meat in the window. There was always a wonderful mouthwatering smell and the sight of the chef in his whites and the succulent joint was the best advert they could have.

Blakemores music shop was another institution and that was where Manx Radio Rentals is now located just on the corner of Fort Street. The properties on the seaward side of Fort Street had a sea wall as their boundary the whole area being tidal before Victoria Street and Loch Promenade were built.

There are still some interesting things to see on some of the buildings if you look hard enough. As we pass the junction with Duke Street look at the building on the corner. Those who are old enough would say 'that's a Burtons shop' and they would be right. Admittedly it was built towards the end of the tramways life but it is interesting to look down at the pavement level and see the foundation stone proclaiming that Raymond Montague Burton himself laid the stone in 1929.

On the left the next large shop was Doyles' Victorian Bazaar (later Gellings Foundry) on the front of which was placed a large statue of

Queen Victoria.   The site has been redeveloped and houses the
administrative offices of Manx Telecom and there with very little
refurbishment needed is Queen Victoria still surveying the street which
bears her name, but from a slightly different vantage point.

Now we have to look up at the top of the buildings still on the left hand
side of the street above the Gas Showroom and there you will see that this
building was the home of the Manx Sun, run by Harriet Curphey, which
was one of the earliest newspapers in the Island and an excellent source
of information to this day. Keep looking but this time on the right hand
side of the street at the top of No 34 just past Thomas Street (next to
Barclays Bank) and observe the inscription. I thought that this was the
establishment of R. Swinnerton, whose address was given as The
Automaton Clock, Victoria Street. His business proudly proclaimed that
it was clockmaker to Her Majesty's Postal Telegraph Dept in the Isle of
Man. I was wrong, however, his establishment was next door to Queen
Victoria a fact pointed out to me by my good friend and local historian
Peter Kelly. No 34 was in fact the establishment of Josiah and William
Goldsmith watchmakers.

Mentioning Barclays Bank reminds me that this site was occupied by
Thomas Street Methodist Church. Thomas Street was severed by Victoria
Street and the church became known as Victoria Street Methodist Church
even though the entrance remained in Thomas Street. It was a magnificent
building and was only demolished in 1977.

As I write this the area occupied by Rosebury Buildings at the foot of
Nelson Street is demolished opening up a view of the Town Hall onto
John Street which I don't think has ever been seen before. The Town Hall
was completed in 1900 and its original entrance was on John Street and
only later changed to Ridgeway Street which was another new street
formed at the same time as Victoria Street. The Douglas Corporation is
celebrating its centenary also in 1996 and as part of the centenary
celebrations the building has recently undergone extensive refurbishment.
At the time that the tramway was being built the whole area must have
been one massive demolition site.

The corner here at the bottom of Prospect Hill was the notorious area
where shopkeepers complained about excessive speed of descending
trams. There were allegations that damage was caused to the sun blinds
in front of the shops. That is something you don't see now, yet if you look
at any of the photographs of the period you will see that the street was
full of shop blinds. As a tall person I certainly remember them vividly! It
is also where in later years the worn state of the pulleys guiding the cable
around the corner rumbled and squealed to the annoyance of all. My
mother used to travel to school by cable car to Mrs Browne's school at
No3 Woodbourne Square and she often spoke of the noise and vibration
from these pulleys.

The tramway and the cable which could be seen below the slot held a
fascination for children.   Young boys would attempt to drop
handkerchiefs or gloves pinched from young girls on the cable. Placing
pennies on the line to see the effect after a tram had passed was another
dangerous pastime. One of my mother's contemporaries lost his leg

through this pursuit.

Imagine two trams passing on the corner or even passing in Victoria Street mixed in with the horse buses and other horsedrawn vehicles and a liberal sprinkling of hand carts and porters carts. It must have been mayhem. Even so it is not all that long ago that the street was two way and double deck buses travelled in both directions mixed in with motor vehicles.

On the left as we start up Prospect Hill are the premises of the National Westminster Bank. At the time of the tramway this was the powerhouse for the financing of all the tramway systems in the Island. It was the building that housed Dumbell's Banking Company, Ltd, with G. W. Dumbell as managing director; Alexander Bruce as general manager and John Shimmon as manager, all key players in the history of the tramways.

Next door Austin Bucknall had his grocery, wines and spirit store a name surviving to the present day still purveying Ales Wines and Spirits and only removed to an adjacent street.

Opposite the bank at No 6 Prospect Hill was the premises of Thos Keig photographer who thankfully recorded much of the contemporary life of Douglas. Another business name that survives to the present day in the town.

A great deal of the hill has been rebuilt although there are still traces of what it was like to be seen on the left hand side. Above Athol Street junction the whole of the right hand side has been completely rebuilt.

On the lower part of Prospect Hill there was the Star Hotel with its largest and best appointed smoke rooms on the Island and where you could, amongst other delights, obtain Bass and Co's best bitter from the barrel and enjoy harmony every evening! A little further up the hill almost exactly opposite Athol Street was the Victoria Hotel with its fifty bedrooms. The hotel we are told boasted coffee, tea, billiard and ladies withdrawing rooms! The ground floor of the hotel fronting onto Prospect Hill was laid out as shops.

At No 16 next door Liborio Hortiguella and John Crellin ran their hairdressing salon 'with best French and English Artistes kept to wait upon customers'. We are also informed that 'on parle Français and se habla Español'. Clearly Douglas was at the forefront of Victorian watering places. Is this the 'those were the days' we all hear about. If so they all seem to me to have had a greater degree of social intercourse.

On the corner of Athol Street is the head office of the Isle of Man Bank. The building was completed in 1902 in an impressive Italianate style and remains imposing and undated to this day.

There is a very interesting photograph on the wall of the new Marks and Spencer store which shows a contemporary view of the lower part of Prospect Hill. Perhaps you should make a point of looking at it after completing the walk.

Now we are approaching the staggered crossroads of Finch Road and Hill Street. This is where the tram tracks diverged and ran closer to the pavement edges now well on opposite sides of the road, as required by the Act. You can't help but be impressed by the equally imposing building on the corner with Finch Road which had been built as the offices of the Bank of Mona but acquired by Government in 1854 and incorporated into new Legislative Buildings by 1894. Prior to this the House of Keys was located at No 11 Athol Street and prior to that in Castletown, the ancient capital of the Island. If the building is open to the public when we are passing it is worth a visit particularly if the Tynwald Court is in session.

On the left is the imposing Roman Catholic church of St Mary of the Isle. The church is part of the Archdiocese of Liverpool and work started on its construction in 1857. Built in the early 13th century French Gothic style to a design by Henry Clutton it was completed just two years later. It was apparently originally intended that the twin towers should have been surmounted by spires. These were not built and the church was finished with one tower having a flat roof and the other having a simple pitched roof giving it a rather odd appearance.

On the right are the main central government buildings and opposite the end of Circular Road the new Law Courts. It was very different when the tramway was operating. The whole of that side of the hill was occupied by town houses. In later years some of the properties were converted to provide shops with living accommodation over, all of which have only disappeared in the last ten years, some even retained their garden walls and railings to the end.

We tend to think that we are just entering a period of dramatic change. Not so, when the tramway was being built many of the properties from now on along the route had not long been built and in fact the further up the hill we go there were large tracts of open country. St Mary's had only been completed thirty seven years earlier and Hill Street and Myrtle Street laid out. Douglas was expanding dramatically. Fortunately our forebears had the foresight to lay out big wide streets with no conception of the traffic that would eventually use them.

The properties on Sydney Mount still present a facade reminiscent of the era.

Now the tramway levelled out somewhat for a short distance passing along Bucks Road in front of a terrace of residences on the right hand side of the road with walled gardens occupying the space now part of the footway. If you look deeper than the shop fronts which now front onto Bucks Road you will see the grand style that these properties once had.

On the left we pass Tynwald Street and Fairfield Terrace with its facade of Victorian boarding houses. Next we come to Finch Hill United Reform Church. Look up at the spire and admire the ornate gargoyles designed with the purely functional purpose of draining rainwater away from the building. A touch more impressive than the plastic rainwater pipes of today! The church was built in 1868.

Now the trams started to climb again and curving past the former Bucks Road Primitive Methodist Church and between the rows of Lodging and Boarding Houses in Bucks Road.

Although these changes in gradient and curvature seem only slight, they contributed to the high maintenance costs of operating the tramway and also caused the noise problems with the cable running hard on the pulleys at these locations causing the pulleys to spin or rumble depending on which side of the road they were located. In addition the cable itself apparently had a tendency to hum and resonate under tension between the pulleys.

Bucks Road levels out as we walk around the curve. The properties have not changed in appearance although their use has changed dramatically. They are really the last bastion of the Victorian street scene in Douglas and probably in need of some tender loving care.

On the left just before we approach Rosemount and the start of Woodbourne Road is the imposing Trinity Methodist Church built in the Gothic style. The foundation stone had been laid in 1886 and although the church was completed by the time of the tramway, the spire was not completed until 1911/12. It is to my mind the most beautiful of all the church spires in the Island and an impressive landmark. You can see that it is a completely separate structure to the church although very carefully and aesthetically linked to it. At the time of the tramway and in fact until comparatively recently the church was known as Rosemount Wesleyan Methodist Church.

Now the tramway really was opening up new ground and contributing to the development of upper Douglas. The introduction of the motor driven omnibus was still some time off. The promoters of the tramway were cashing in on the development having seen the potential of the visitors staying in the considerable number of lodging and boarding houses which had been built since 1880. They were providing the essential link with the Victoria Pier which was the point of entry for almost all of the visitors arriving on the Island. The place, to use modern jargon, was really buzzing.

The Rosemount Hotel is No 1 Woodbourne Road although it is also No 1 Adelaide Terrace. photographs of cablecars on Prospect Terrace do more than words to adequately describe the scene. But still if you look closely at the buildings on either side of the road you will see that some of them retain very much of their original character. Look at Prospect Terrace, built in a late Regency style. The pavement in front of the shops was much wider at the time that the tramway was built. If you look carefully at the terrace you will be able to see the original extent of it as built.

Trees overhung the left hand side of the road and if you look up the lane between Adelaide Terrace and Stephen Terrace there is still some hint of the rural roots of the area to be seen. When the tramway was being built many of the streets beyond here were still being laid out and constructed.

Now we are in Woodbourne Road and there is No 3 Woodbourne Square. This must have been where my mother got off the tram to go to school. Here is confusion because the nameplate on the building proclaims that this is indeed Woodburn Square and yet a similar cast iron nameplate tells us that we are in Woodbourne Road. I have no idea which is correct other than to say that both are shown as Woodbourne on the maps and in the Directory.

When these houses were built and the streets laid out the developers laid out a number of formal squares and gardens. I think that they are absolutely wonderful. But then I am prejudiced because as a young lad I used to play in this one and at the time it was somewhat overgrown due to the restrictions imposed by wartime. I also used to eat wonderful Chelsea buns from Oates and Quayle's shop in the square with my pals usually after watching the Saturday matinee at the Strand Cinema and overdosed on cowboys and indians but that is another story!

Lets make a detour. We won't miss anything by walking through the gardens. I hope that the palms are in full bloom when you are there because I often refer to this small park as our 'Kew Gardens' and I am sure you will see why.

From now on the tramway was travelling through an area where only sporadic development had taken place. It was the domain of the wealthy.

Leaving West View, look to the right and you will see the Masonic Hall. This was not its guise when the tramway reached here. It was Woodbourne House and in fact its basic shape is still there to be seen if you look at the main entrance through the gates on the corner. Most of upper Douglas was built on land from the Woodbourne Estate. Just behind the Masonic Hall you can see another of those delightful town squares that I mentioned. Hilary Park is totally different in character to Woodbourne Square.

Back to the route of the tramway. The rows of houses on the left are all built in terraces and each is named but regrettably the names no longer appear on the houses. There was Earl Terrace, followed by Burnside Terrace and Alexander Terrace that seems to want to go straight on and not follow the line of the road. Was there a scheme to re-align the road? I don't know but it certainly looks like it. Woodside Terrace, on the opposite side of the road, was there in 1896 and Woodside House, which occupied the site of the present Mormon Church.

The tramway ran downhill to the corner where Albany Road joins Woodbourne Road, starting to climb again as it negotiated the corner continuing to climb to its highest point at Avondale, with Salisbury Terrace and Newsome Terrace just recently laid out and building work in progress.

The crossover added in 1927 was located just before we reach Holmfield, now the offices of the Dept of Home Affairs, which is the imposing residence on the right behind the high stone wall.

The tramway was now pioneering in open country. Beyond Avondale there were fields and photographs exist which can help us appreciate this fact. There is a classic one showing cablecar No 73 negotiating Avondale with recently completed houses on the end of Newsome Terrace and nothing beyond.

The tramway negotiated a sharp corner here to enter what later became York Road. Just before the corner the twin tracks joined into a single line (doubled in 1905) to negotiate the corner and remained like that as it descended to the depot which was built on open ground with the winding house alongside.

From the traffic lights at Avondale corner turn right into York Road. There were few houses built here in 1896 and contemporary photographs bear out this fact. We pass Laureston Avenue on the right and this is where the tram drivers let go of the cable to coast into the entrance to the depot which was served by the traverser.

Lets sit on the seat by the flower garden on the left before we walk into Ballaquayle Road. In front of us is the Waverley Court sheltered housing built on the site of the depot, which after 1921 was used to house the Douglas Corporation bus fleet (refer to photograph). To the left was the winding house and the cable came out into the roadway through a tunnel into a system of tensioning pulleys and diverter pulleys which turned the cable through 90 degrees to pull up Broadway and down York Road (see diagram). Those pulleys still exist but are now buried under the road. There was a time when the tunnel was used as a rifle range by a local club and you could just squeeze into the end chamber and see the pulleys. You can see them on the photograph I took some years ago. Now the diverter pit is almost under your feet and buried under the road.

The tramway was nothing if not ambitious as it now continued downhill turning right into Ballaquayle Road with Waverley Terrace on the right and Stanley View on the left. The next road on the right is Waverley Road. If you look at the road surface you will see some tram lines just showing through the surface. This is now just about the only visible remains of the cable tramway system. This was the track which was used to take horse trams into the shed which was built in the yard adjoining the old boiler house. The surviving cablecar was assembled from the two cars used as a bungalow at the Killane in this shed.

Continuing down Ballaquayle Road we are again into terraces of houses. Stanley View is still on the left with Drury Terrace on the right followed by Clifton Terrace all Victorian style boarding houses. Opposite Clifton Terrace are some much older houses which form Stanley Terrace and built in a late Tudor style.

Now the cable tramway entered Broadway which was anything but broad. On the right was the walled garden surrounding Glen Falcon House which was only demolished in 1948 when the opportunity was taken to widen Broadway and lay out Glen Falcon gardens. The route here was steep and with several curves all of which added friction to the cable. It was as Keith has described the straw that broke the camel's back! The tramway was shortened as early as 1902 to Stanley View just upside of the junction of Marathon Road with Ballaquayle Road.

Carry on down Broadway and observe Sherwood Terrace on the left with the Broadway Baptist Church built in 1893 followed by more Victorian houses ending with the Central Hotel and the Promenade.

On the right was Villa Marina Mansion but not the entertainment building that we see now. It was the site of the private residence of Henry Bloom Noble and surrounded by a high stone wall. the Villa Marina house and grounds were only purchased by the Douglas Corporation some years after the tramway terminus had been moved to Stanley View.

It is not clear where the terminal pit was located at Broadway but it is fair to assume that it must have been somewhere opposite the entrance to the Central Hotel and in the centre of the road.

That then is the route of the cable tramway in its entirety. I suggest that you return to the starting point by the Promenade where work is in progress to refurbish and modernise the town's sewage disposal system which was built at the time of the tramway having been designed by Mr Stevenson borough engineer of Halifax and work had commenced in 1866. If that is not your particular interest you could return through Strand Street which is the main shopping street of the town and don't forget to slip into Marks and Spencers to look at those photographs.

A WALK ALONG THE ROUTE OF THE DOUGLAS SOUTHERN ELECTRIC TRAMWAY

This walk is best done in the morning, otherwise sections of it will be in shadow and not seen to best advantage. We shall start this walk also from the Jubilee Clock as it is a convenient starting point. It had been the intention to bring the proposed tramway around Douglas harbour to a point near here as shown on Keith's sketch of the 1895-97 extension proposals.

We shall head off along Walpole Avenue which is the road leading off at right angles to the promenade. It emerges in Parade Street with the bus station on our right and the I.o.M. Steam Packet Co. warehouse on the left (the site of the proposed tower to carry the suspension bridge that never materialised).

Cross the road with care to the warehouses and follow Parade Street to the Douglas Harbour Swing Bridge, which we shall walk across. The present bridge structure dates from the early 1980s replacing the original bridge which was built in 1895.

The original bridge weighed 450 tons and was built by Armstrong-Mitchell of Newcastle upon Tyne. It was 24ft wide and was operated as a toll bridge for vehicles up to 2 tons in weight as well as for pedestrians. The bridge was operated by hydraulic power from an accumulator housed in the tower on the opposite side of the harbour. The mechanism still exists and operates the present pedestrian only bridge.

We cross the bridge and you will see as we walk on to it the original toll booths. We turn left as soon as we leave the bridge and walk along the Approach Road which is on the south side of the harbour giving access to the Douglas Breakwater. The road was built some thirty years before the tramway on the Marine Drive.

A short distance along the road just before it widens we pass the site of the former Fort Anne Hotel on the right. It was originally the home of Sir William Hillary and he was the founder of the Society for the Preservation of Life from Shipwreck which later became the Royal National Lifeboat Institution. When he lived at Fort Anne the harbour was very much different than what we see now. This area was exposed to the full force of the sea with no shelter and it was the high incidence of shipwreck virtually on his front door that moved Sir William to promote his lifesaving society.

The next point of interest as we walk towards the Breakwater is the present lifeboat house. In Sir William's time the first lifeboat house was located in the vicinity of Broadway and the lifeboat launched from the beach. If the boathouse is open it is worth going inside to have a look at some of the records inside and at the boat itself which appropriately is named after the founder of the lifeboat service. The present Tyne class lifeboat is far removed from the sailing and pulling boats of 1826 which was the date of the first lifeboat to be stationed on the Island. I think that Sir William would have been impressed.

We carry on to the breakwater and turn right passing the former harbour yard and the Shell terminal. Did you notice the rails in the roadway? Very little of them remain now and every time some resurfacing work is carried out more are removed. You will have seen that they are ten foot gauge and were for the 25-ton Cowans and Sheldon steam crane which for many years was the only heavy lift facility at Douglas.

Look at the plaques on the end of the breakwater and you will read a potted history of the harbour. The plaques are actually mounted on the wave wall of the Battery Pier which now forms part of the new breakwater. You will see also from the inscription that the formal name of the new breakwater is the Princess Alexandra Pier.

Walk up the hill past the Coastguard Headquarters, which incidentally used to be a café, and round onto the flat area above known locally as the quarter deck. Now the reason for this apparent detour can be seen. Standing with your back to the breakwater you will see the formation of the Douglas Head Incline Railway. Built four years after the Douglas Southern to connect the harbour ferries with Douglas Head and the Marine Drive it outlasted the Marine Drive Tramway being eventually dismantled in 1955.

The whole of this area was a hive of activity at the time of the tramway with bathing at Port Skillion in a pool constructed between the Little Head where we are standing and Douglas Head where the lighthouse is built. There were fortune tellers, amusements and stalls selling seafood and fancy goods. There was also a set of elaborate brass weighing scales which also lasted into the 1950s on which you could get weighed. We must not forget the Camera Obscura just above us. I can remember many times going into its dark interior and being fascinated by the moving pictures presented each viewing position and watching the trams on the funicular incline. One view in particular showed the trams crossing the footpath that we must now climb.

Nothing else for it I'm afraid we have to climb the steps in front of us alongside the formation of the incline railway. Take a breather halfway up and admire the view over Douglas Bay. You can also see below you the outer breakwater completed in 1985 and behind the gas storage tank you can see the Battery Pier completed in 1879 which had been for over a hundred years the breakwater providing protection for Douglas harbour. It having replaced an Abernethy type breakwater dating from 1864.

The path now swings under the route of the incline railway and passes the Camera Obscura which has now passed into Government ownership and destined for preservation. Up the final flights of steps and we arrive at Head Road. To our right was the upper station of the incline railway which housed the oil engine which provided the power for the cable and winding gear. Ahead of us was the Douglas terminus of the Douglas Southern Electric Tramway.

The road was much narrower than today and the tramway was on the side of the road nearest the cliff face.

Now we are on the route of the tramway which was built on the Marine Drive which as you will already have read pre-dated the tramway by some four years. Although its ultimate completion became inexorably entangled with the tramway itself.

Starting off along the Marine Drive we swing right with the Drive probably as near to its original state as you will find anywhere. The tramway ran against the cliff face and the small wall with the ornate railing referred to by Keith still exists in its original form for a short distance between here and the tollgate.

Just before we reach the tollgate we cross the first of the half bridges which were built on the original Drive. This was replaced in 1955 still as a half bridge, but with the original iron girders being replaced by concrete beams.

At the tollgate the arches still remain, but the house and office have long since been demolished. You can, however, still see the location of the turnstile as you walk on the footpath through the original pedestrian entrance. There were elaborate wrought iron gates at these openings and for many years they lay at the Quarterbridge Depot of the Highway Board. They may still exist but I don't know where.

Until comparatively recently one of the insulators and suspensions that carried the overhead through the inner arch could be seen. That too seems to have succumbed to the ravages of time.

After the Drive came into Government ownership considerable sections were widened such as the section we are presently walking along. It is possible to make out the formation of the tramway on the landward side in places. Widening did not take place on the double corners which follow and we can still see some of the original features including the castlellated walls and railings and half bridges where the original steelwork on one can still be seen.

Next we approach the embankment at Pigeon's Stream with its adjoining car park. The tramway crossed this valley with a triple span lattice girder bridge. The Highway Board collapsed the bridge by explosives and then filled the area with excavated material to form the present embankment in 1956. Some of the fill material came from the power station which was demolished at the same time. The site of the power station has now been turned into a small car park. If you walk onto the car park area you will be able to make out the outline of the main masonry walls of the building and some of the concrete floor at this level.

Before leaving this area take a look towards the headland in the distance. You will see the bulky outline of the Howe and the route of the marine drive cut into the cliff and below the roadway a pointed rock. This is the rock known as the Nuns' Chairs.* The two distinct ledges on the seaward side of this rock are reputed to be places where Nuns from the nearby Nunnery were required to serve penance. I am not sure if there is truth in this story or whether the rock was purely a fishing mark and so named by the fishermen because of the resemblance to a chair and the fact that it was on what was part of the Nunnery Estate.

*D.S.E.T.'s notice made this a singular 'furnishing'!

Continuing our walk we immediately pass an inlet known as Quirks

Cove and again you will see the original boundary wall protecting the edge of the footway. The tramway was on the landward side of the road and climbed steadily to Wallberry Head in the distance. In places particularly on the corners traces of the formation of the tramway can be seen and there are more traces of the original boundary walls.

Now we have reached the headland we could see in the distance. Just before we round the corner stop and look up to the right. The stone built building, now minus its roof, was an explosives magazine for Todhunter and Elliot one of the principal suppliers of explosives in the Island. Note the double walls with the space between which was a distinct characteristic of such buildings. If you look back along the route of the tramway you can see the tollgate in the far distance. Imagine what an exhilarating ride it must have been on a tram! Well if you think that might have been impressive just wait till you get around the corner.

We are now approaching Wallberry meaning hawks' cliff one of the many place names in the Island left to us by our Scandinavian forebears. The Viking name for the place was Valaberg and what we have now is the anglicised corruption of the word.

This was the first obstacle to confront the promoters of the original marine drive. Not only did they have the steep formidable cliff, but a yawning chasm. They eventually chose to cut their road into the cliff round the first right hand corner and then following the natural curve of the cliff to the left they then built a timber trestle bridge across the gorge. The northern abutment can just be seen from the present roadway where the road swings right again to curve around the natural bowl of Wallberry.

The bridge was built in two spans with a centre pier built on top of a natural rock outcrop now nearly covered by the fill material tipped over the side of the new roadway as it was cut into the cliff.

You can also see, as we walk around the present roadway, the masonry of the southern abutment. Just as we reach the point above the abutment stop and look back across the ravine. This is the alignment of the original road and the tramway. The wooden bridge was replaced by the Douglas Southern Electric as you will see from the photographs. What is not always apparent is the fact that there was a quite noticeable bend in the bridge dictated purely by the alignment of the solid foundation for the central pier and the two points of entry at either side. From here you should be able to see the problem facing those early builders.

It was no easier in the late 1950s when the Highway Board were faced with the problem of resurrecting the Marine Drive. The condition and width of the existing bridges precluded their use. Cost evaluation both of construction and subsequent maintenance led to the conclusion that the cheapest and best solution was to continue the original concept of cutting a roadway into the cliff using modern blasting techniques.

The firm of Messrs John Brown of Wolverhampton were subsequently employed to carry out the necessary work. The contorted rock strata of the area, mostly slate, proved to be extremely difficult to work and the rock ledge was cut with great difficulty. Also as a cost saving measure the spoil from the excavation was tipped over the side of the cliff to form additional support to the edge of the carriageway. Proposed sea defences to the foot of this fill material, most of which you can see below the road, were omitted as a further cost saving exercise. This was to prove to be a costly mistake. A further blow would be dealt by nature with the vertical bedding plane of the rock.

Continuing our walk we find ourselves on a short fairly level straight section where cutting the original formation would have been relatively easy. It was here that Wallberry passing loop was constructed at the end nearest the Wallberry bridge and you can see clearly where it was constructed.

A short distance brings us to the site of the third bridge at Horseleap which spanned this difficult gully in one span between the two masonry abutments which can still be clearly seen. The present road was cut into the cliff using the same principle as at Wallberry. Here more clearly than anywhere else can be seen the disastrous effect of not providing the sea defence to the toe of the fill material. Successive south easterly gales eroded the material to such an extent that the outer edge of the road was affected and this was what eventually led to the closure of the Drive to vehicular traffic. At this location also the rock strata encountered was probably the worst on the whole job.

The verticality of the strata allowed the ingress of water which froze every winter causing the fissures to open and that coupled with the stress relief in the rock caused by the removal of the overburden resulted in considerable rockfalls. This area also proved to be the most difficult for two way bus traffic.

As far as the tramway was concerned it simply leapt across this chasm with nothing but the sea below. My mother recalled the first time she travelled over these bridges on the top deck of a tram as extremely frightening! I think it would have certainly been an experience you would not forget in a hurry particularly on the open top of a four wheeled tram. Imagine travelling towards Douglas sitting on the right hand side on the top deck and looking over the edge down to the sea below with the noise of the tram on the bridge echoing off the cliff. It would certainly have been worth the money!

Now the Drive comes into more open country with the cliff a little less hostile. Immediately round the corner you will see more clearly than anywhere else the formation of a passing place. We are now approaching the area where the depot was located. The headland out to our left is Little Ness. We shall have to take care again because this section of the Drive has recently been reopened to traffic and the depot area made available for car parking.

As we approach the area we can see where the tramway would have crossed the road to gain access to the depot. Reference to the photographs should help. If we go down into the area and look carefully to the right as we walk down you will see another of the few remaining signs of the tramway. There under the gorse are the pits which were in the car shed and used for servicing the trams. Be careful you don't fall when looking for them.

Carry on along the Drive which follows the original formation for a short distance until the alignment skirts the head of an inlet. Look over the fence and you will see a square shaped inlet with a large cave on the southern flank. The area as far as I can determine does not seem to have a local name. Ahead of us there is some spoil from the work carried out when the drive was widened and if you look you will see some rusted remnants of steel sleepers from the tramway. Many of them were used for fencing but they have all rusted away and none remain other than the odd rusted stump here and there.

The next point of interest is the Whing. You can't miss it because quite suddenly we are back amongst the contorted strata and high rock faces with very fragmented rock. The new road has been cut into the cliff here obliterating the original tramway formation but it would have looked somewhat similar. There were, and still are some small half bridges spanning small clefts in the rock on the seaward side of the road. Subsidence has occurred here caused by surface water erosion which has been a problem since the drive was originally built.

Walking around the sweep on the Whing we quickly approach another inlet. Now we are at Rebog, another Scandinavian place name which occurs frequently in the Island. Sometimes spelt Rheboeg and derived from Ripvik meaning rocky creek. Look over the wall by the seat and you will be able to see the remains of a Dutch coaster Grietje which ran aground in a snowstorm in 1961. The crew were all rescued by the Coastguard cliff rescue team.

As we leave Rebog you will observe that the roadway has been moved in from the cliff edge. This was a direct result of such erosion. The photograph showing the two buses passing was taken at this location before the roadway was realigned.

Now it is all downhill round a series of bends to Keristal yet another derivation of a Norse name referring to Rock Farm or Ballacregga as it is now named. Keristal was the original terminus of the tramway, although the Drive continued to Oakhill and the original timber framed and galvanised sheet steel clad gatehouse still stands. The building was purchased as a standard gentleman's shooting lodge and erected by the Marine Drive Company as a toll gate house and residence for their foreman. I remember being proudly shown this document by his daughter Mrs Marshall who had lived there all her life and an infinite fount of knowledge about the Drive.

As you will have read, the glen at Keristal was filled in and an embankment formed and the tramway extended towards Port Soderick very shortly after the opening.

Follow the roadway round the curve over the embankment. This is the route of the tramway as it continued for a further threequarters of a mile to the Port Soderick terminus. As we walk along the footway it is worth stopping to look back along the route over Keristal at Rebog and the Whing. The gradient which gave the inspectors so much heartache in relation to the brake operation can be clearly seen from here. In the far distance you can also see the headland of Little Ness. If you look inland at the fields you will become aware of the proximity of the Isle of Man Steam Railway Line. When the tramway was being built the railway was already in place and served Port Soderick as we shall see a little later.

As we walk along the footpath look out for the public right of way sign directing us to Port Soderick down the grassy pathway.

This was the terminus of the tramway by the spring of 1897. It is difficult to imagine just how it was as there was no roadway. Passengers having got off the tram had to walk along the path and down the steps to the entertainment at Port Soderick just as we are doing.

As you will have read, Mr Forrester built a cliff lift to help potential patrons to gain access to his establishment. It became operational in 1898 and in fact as we start to descend the steps you might still be able to make out some of the supports for the headgear. As we walk down the steps the piers which carried the track are quite apparent as the steps follow the line of the lift to the promenade.

Having now reached Port Soderick we can sample the hospitality of The Anchor whilst contemplating our return to Douglas. This is where the timetable that I suggested you bring will come in handy. We can walk back the way we came, or we can walk back a different way, or use the bus or the steam railway. Whatever you decide we have to continue along the promenade and into the glen. Follow the pathway through the glen alongside the stream until we join a well defined track. Sharp right here and up to the roadway to turn left and under the bridge that carries the railway. If the railway is your choice for return to Douglas then follow the sign to the station up the track which is on the left just as we emerge from under the bridge.

If you intend to walk back or catch the bus then continue uphill until the Old Castletown Road is reached. Turn right and head for Port Soderick village which is about half a mile away. You are now on the bus route and can catch a Douglas bound bus at one of the wayside halts. Be careful to consult the timetable because the service is infrequent.

For those of us keen to walk back to Douglas we must look out for a signpost leading off to the left as we reach the village. It is on the corner as we approach the village hall. The signpost indicates a footpath to Kewaigue and that is where we shall go.

The track is narrow at first but comes to a junction with a wider surfaced road after about another half mile. Go straight across taking care not to go down the private drive. This is Middle Farm road and is an old public highway leading across what is affectionately known locally as the Giant's Belly.

Across the valley on our right is the Howe and the Carnanes with the prominent communication masts. On the other side of that high ground is the Marine Drive where we walked earlier.

Soon we come to Middle Farm itself and emerge onto a surfaced road at Kewaigue almost opposite the school. Cross the road with care as the traffic will not be expecting us to emerge from the gateway.

We make our way down the hill alongside the Municipal Golf Course almost to the railway bridge which carries the railway over the road. Just before we reach it and just a little further than the pavement, there is yet another footpath leading off to the left beside a small stream. The stream is the Middle River and the path runs alongside it through a wooden glen. Not so idyllic as it seems as it once was the main refuse tip for the town of

Douglas. Still we fairly quickly emerge alongside the golf course in the open and very close to the action. We are not in any danger but it is wise to keep our wits about us just in case!

As we approach the clubhouse we join another track which crosses the stream over a concrete bridge. Turn right here and follow the track which skirts the trees and the railway cutting at the Nunnery which is on our right. Then suddenly we cross under the railway which is carried on a steel girder bridge across the track and the Douglas River.

Continue along the track which is more defined now and is also an old road the route of which can be clearly traced from Douglas to Old Kirk Braddan Church. Along the way there is a break in the wall on our right which forms the boundary to the Nunnery Estate. If we stop we can read a little about a previous owner of the Nunnery Estate and his exploits in the Crimean War.

A short distance further and we come out onto the Old Castletown Road. Follow the river and walk along Leigh Terrace to the harbour and we are back in Douglas almost where we started. Turn left and cross the Douglas Bridge which as you will read was completed in 1937 replacing the earlier two arched stone bridge. Complete the walk by following the South Quay and we are back in Parade Street by the bus station and the full circle completed.

Surviving headgear of the Port Soderick lift.
Stan Basnett

Appendix The Cliff Lifts

The two Incline Railways now to be described played a major role in D.S.E.T./D.H.M.D. operation. In order of construction they were:

(i) Port Soderick Holiday Beach Lift

Forrester family development here reached its zenith in the construction of an elegant curved promenade, still carrying a datestone inscribed 'Erected by M. & T. Forrester, 1897', and in the construction of a lift to link the beach with the new Marine Drive tramway. This was the 1887 Falcon Cliff lift,* re-erected in the same basic form, with 4-in deep Vignoles rails laid to 4-ft gauge on parallel 12in by 12in timbers at centres of 4ft 2in, 2ft 9in and 4ft 2in respectively. Some new material was used, the line being substantially longer than at Douglas.

Two new cars were provided, builder unknown: with inclined turtleback roofs they must have been a bodybuilder's nightmare. The drive was now by an oil engine driving a cable of 3$^{1}/_{2}$in circumference. An oddly-shaped corrugated-iron building housed the engine and head gear, still partly *in situ,* and a top loading platform, whose characteristic iron fence and twin gateways also survive. Lower down, expensive timber viaduct construction was involved; the ivy-clad stone pillars remain today. As earlier, the cars were sloped to match the lift's gradient, and at the bottom end of their run entered a terminal station, later given an all-over roof, built about 1902 to the same slope.

P. Nevill, Harbour Board engineer, gave his inspector's approbation on 9 July 1898 after making six visits. He had reported to the governor on 25 June that he was far from happy with the installation – whilst the cars were new, little else was.   The governor's secretary wrote on 11 July 1898 giving final approval for working to commence.

Final closure can be assumed concurrent with that of the Marine Drive tramway in September 1939. In 1946 it was sold with the hotel, and was dismantled between 1947 and 1949. A footpath which offered an alternative way down was later rebuilt. The cars survived

The early livery of the Port Soderick 'Holiday Beach Lift' cars seems to have been a highly elaborate affair, on the evidence of this revealing photograph. With their demise (see text) all possible evidence was lost.

Courtesy Manx National Heritage

---

*See the Author's 'Isle of Man Tramways' (David and Charles, 1970).

An August 1953 photograph of the Douglas Head Incline Railway shows the line in its final operational year. The second view is taken looking down the incline and clearly shows the intermediate bend. The cars were then green, silver and white. In the late 'twenties a more traditional livery included a roof board whose lettering announced 'Cars to Marine Drive & Top of Head'. The actual colours are unknown. The twin funnelled Edwardian 'racer', 'Viking' (seen at the breakwater pier) had but one further year of service ahead of her.

J. N. Slater and the Author

into the post-war years as henhouses, until some cattle poisoned themselves by chewing the lead paint from the canvas of their roofs!

(ii) Douglas Head Incline Railway

On 21 January 1898 an agreement was concluded between Sir John Goldie-Taubman and R. M. Broadbent for a 'double or single mechanical tramway or lift or railway and lift combined with necessary crossings and loops' from a point near the Battery pier to a point to seaward of the Douglas Southern tramway on Douglas Head. Promoted by R. M. Broadbent of Ivydene, Douglas, this took shape in 1900 as a double-track funicular, typically of 4ft gauge,

Rubbing taken from the Hurst Nelson builders plate of a DHIR car. *Author*

extending from a lower station at the rear of Douglas Head lighthouse near Port Skillion to a combined upper terminal building and engine house not far from the DSET terminus, and passing over a footpath en route. The inclination was 1 in 4½ over the entire length of 450ft, with a bend about one-third of the way up, and the double track (laid in 70lb flat bottom rail) was close together on the lower section and further apart higher up (where the cars passed). Motive power was an oil engine, housed in the basement of the upper terminal. In July 1900, two inclined railway cars (drawing 5072/25) were supplied by Hurst Nelson & Co of Motherwell, and the line assumedly opened later that summer. Operation thereafter was seasonal.

On 7 July 1922, the line was sold by Broadbent and his wife to Douglas Head Incline Railway Ltd, whose office was at the upper station. A Nunnery estate deed of 30 June 1926, includes the requirement to operate from the Friday before Whit Monday until September 30. The lift was closed during the two wars, and re-commenced operation about 1949 – the writer used it in 1950 – but ran only for the next five seasons, and by August 1954 it lay disused. According to A. M. Goodwyn the lift changed hands in 1940 and again in 1947. Liquidation in 1954 was followed by winding up on 15 October 1956. It was meanwhile dismantled in October and November of 1955, the rails being relaid on the MER approaching Ramsey. Little now remains.

The closure was a direct consequence of a competing Corporation bus service to Douglas Head and the resulting starvation of the ferry service to the foot of the lift. A rather pathetic letter from the proprietors of <u>Douglas Head Ferries Ltd</u> to the town council, dated 22 February 1950, asked that their previous monopoly be left undisturbed for a further period now that two steamers were available, but this met with no response and the buses to the Head ran from 1950. During 1949, the corporation had tried to run a service along the south side of the harbour to the cliff lift. In its heyday, the steam ferry fleet comprised three vessels, *Thistle, Rose* and *Shamrock;* one of the trio was sold after the war, but sank en route for the (mainland) breakers. The other two remained in Douglas until the last being broken up c.1966-7.

Bibliography

Whilst the Douglas Southern's detail story is only traceable through the press references already indicated, the 'technology' of cable tramways has been made more accessible through reprints and specialist historical studies. In the former category are:

(i) 'A Treatise upon Cable or Rope Traction as Applied to the Working of Street and Other Railways'
Owlswick Press (Philadelphia), 1977 (Author Bucknall Smith, 1887, reprint with additions by G.W. Hilton, 1977)

(ii) 'The Cable System of Tramway Traction'
Mechanical Traction Syndicate, 1896 (Reprint by Adam Gordon, 1994).

In the latter category the salient works are:

(i) 'The Cable Car in America'
Howell-North Books   (Author Prof. G.W. Hilton)

(ii) Edinburgh Transport (Author D.L.G. Hunter, M.I. Mech.E.)
Advertiser Press, 1964

See also 'The Dick Kerr Story' by J.H. Price (T&LRS, 1995)

Acknowledgements

The main sources used in compiling this work, other than personal interview and correspondence, have been the Manx Press, the transport and technical Press, and official reports. The first comprise The *Isle of Man Examiner, The Isle of Man Times, The Manxman,* and *Mona's Herald,* the second *The Engineer, Electrical Review, The Electrician, The Light Railway and Tramway Journal, Modern Tramway, Railway Magazine, The Street Railway Journal,* and *Tramway and Railway World* (formerly *Railway World*). The reports consulted are those of Douglas Corporation, the Select Committees of Tynwald, and, particularly, of the Inspectors acting on behalf of the Manx Government at the inception of the two lines concerned. Material housed in the Rolls Office and in Government Office (in whose location the late E.C. Shimmin played a major role), and in the British Museum Newspaper Library and the Public Record Office, and the (then) Companies Registration Office of the Board of Trade all played a part in the completion of this text. Reference has already been made to the use of papers then (1968) held by the Nunnery Estate, by permission of the late Captain J.W.L. Fry-Goldie Taubman. Miss Ann Harrison (then of the Manx Museum) was able to locate valuable new material on both lines.

In the years before 1970 major help from the following individuals played a vital role. Sadly, this acknowledgement is a posthumous one in the present day context. Those concerned were Inspector Jack Dugdale, Joint Controllers A. Hampton and D. Halsall, Surveyor General R.C.W. Brown, W.A. Camwell and R.B. Parr, S.H. Davenport, R. Elliot, Messrs J. and J. Knox, J.D. Craine, George Lace, M.J. O'Connor, Rev. Bertram Kelly, Reginald Orton and family, W.E. Vick, Miss G.H. Pitt, Mrs. M. Marshall, Tom Cowley and the Nunnery Agent, O.S. Wrangham. Happily, the former Director of the Manx Museum, B.R.S. Megaw, is still with us.

Companies who assisted in the early 1950's were Bellis and Morcom, Heenan and Froude and Westinghouse International.

For work during the present year I am indebted to Stan Basnett, Keith Burbage, Captain Stephen Carter, John C. Cooke, Carey Graff Baker, Stephen Broomfield, R.J.S. Wiseman, Paul Abell, Peter Hammond, Wilson Gibb and Adam Gordon, also the Librarian Archivist of Manx National Heritage, Roger Sims B,A, D.A.A. and the Archivists of the Institutions of Civil and Electrical Engineers. Sections of this text dating from 1968 were edited with characteristic expertise (and additional research input) by John H. Price, and a special 'thank you' is due to D.W.K. Jones for his excellent photo record of events on 23 June, 1951.

The Cable Car Group's 1977 booklet 'Cable Car Days' contains a extensive list of the individuals and undertakings who assisted in the 'rescue and rehabilitation' outlined in the present text. Now, almost twenty years later the vehicle continues to enjoy the hospitality of Douglas Corporation, a debt which requires no emphasis. Their cooperation during the most recent operations using battery power equally deserves especial mention, coupled with personal thanks to Mr. Peter Cannon, and to long standing friend Derek Shepherd for his technical wizardry in producing a viable scheme ('aided and abetted' by Maurice Faragher!). Over the previous years, the expertise in Land Rover propulsion acquired by Donald Whittaker saw some memorable runs, with (latterly) highly developed safety flagman techniques as accompaniment, courtesy Mike Tucker.

Tailpiece: 'Thistle' as seen in 1934 (see p.132). These vessels had four propellors and boasted two rudders, being fully bi-directional. Two were taken to the Dardanelles in 1915, and, all in all, their history is deserving of a detailed account.

The late B.Y. Williams

Index

INDEX

ADDENDA

INDEX, CHAPTER 4